A GREAT G

A GREAT
GULF FIXED

SERMONS ON THE RICH MAN AND LAZARUS

A Practical Exposition
of Luke xvi., 19-31

BROWNLOW NORTH

THE BANNER OF TRUTH TRUST

THE BANNER OF TRUTH TRUST
3 Murrayfield Road, Edinburgh EH12 6EL
PO Box 621, Carlisle, Pennsylvania 17013, USA

*

First Banner of Truth Trust Edition,
The Rich Man and Lazarus, 1960

Reprinted 1961
Reprinted 1964
Reprinted 1968
Reprinted 1979
Reprinted as *A Great Gulf Fixed* 1999

ISBN 0 85151 765 X

*

Printed in Finland by WSOY

CONTENTS

	PAGE
INTRODUCTION	7
EARTHLY SUFFERING NOT SALVATION	13
HOW THE BEGGAR BECAME RICH	25
HOW THE RICH MAN BECAME POOR	35
THE POOR RICH MAN	49
HE PRAYS	59
GOD THE ONLY HEARER OF PRAYER	70
EARNEST, HEART-FELT, TOO-LATE PRAYER ...	79
THE ANSWER	87
THE SECOND PETITION	101
SIX SHORT RULES FOR YOUNG CHRISTIANS ...	116

ARE YOU ASLEEP? AN ADDRESS BY J. C. RYLE ... 117

INTRODUCTION

TOWARDS the end of June, 1859, two men paced the deck of a vessel bound from Greenock to Northern Ireland. It was a fine summer evening and in the fading light the purple grandeur of the surrounding mountains and the dark water of the Clyde were an impressive sight. But the attention of the two passengers was doubtless absorbed with other things for this was to be no ordinary visit they were paying to Ulster. It is in the shorter of the two men that we are interested—a man of strong features, broad shouldered, deep chested and striking in bearing. Forty-nine years of age and wearing the dark clothes of a country gentleman, there was nothing to indicate to his fellow passengers the purpose of his crossing. And even Brownlow North himself did not know the momentous consequences that were to issue from it.

In all the annals of biography, there is hardly a more interesting story than the life of Brownlow North. His grandfather, the Bishop of Winchester, was the son of Lord North—an eighteenth-century prime minister and parliamentary leader. Thus from his birth in 1810, Brownlow North was surrounded by aristocratic connections and church dignitaries. In his six years at Eton he was known as "Gentleman Jack" and distinguished himself as an athlete rather than a scholar. Once his school days were over, he soon settled down to a life of leisure, and while always professing the religion of his family, his pastimes clearly indicated where his pleasures lay; riding, shooting, billiards and dancing, these were the things upon which he set his heart.   Sometimes, it is true, he had some serious thoughts, as, for instance, when a friend with whom he was racing on horse-back was killed at his side by a stage coach, or when a word of advice from the Duchess of Gordon sobered him, but these things made no lasting impression on his lightheartedness.   Let us hear him tell his own story :

" For forty-four years of my life, my object was to pass time pleasantly; so long as the day was spent agreeably I was satisfied.   During those years, whatever harm I may have done, I do not believe I ever did any real good to a human being.   From 1835 until 1854, with the exception of about three years, the greater part of my time was spent in Scotland, where I rented moors and fisheries.   My greatest idea of pleasure was to shoot grouse and catch salmon.

" I believe, at the different shooting quarters I rented, I treated the poor with an average liberality,—contributing to the different collections what I fancied would be expected, with an odd five shillings when an old woman lost her cow; but what I considered my great act of kindness to the people, and that for which I expected them to be most thankful, was to give them, at the end of the shooting season, a dance and supper.

Now let not the philanthropist imagine that I intend to compare his philanthropy with mine. I put his on the very highest scale, mine on the very lowest: only maintaining, that to the recipients of our kindnesses it will be all the same a hundred years hence.

" To this party of mine all the tenants in the neighbourhood, with their wives and their daughters, were invited; as also the gamekeepers, the gillies, the shopkeepers of the village, my own servants, and all and sundry, and every acquaintance that any of these liked to bring. They were very merry. Late in the evening perhaps some were very noisy; and early in the morning I have seen some very tipsy. It would be daylight, perhaps, when a number of both sexes, giving me three cheers, and thanking me for my kindness, would cry,— ' God bless you,' and start on their ways home.

" They thanked me for my kindness; but was it kindness? They cried, ' God bless me!' but could either they or I expect God's blessing on such a meeting? It is true it was intended kindly, and as a return for kindness to those who had taken care of my shootings and preserved my game, and I knew no better way of saying, ' I am much obliged to you '; yet again I ask, ' Was it kindness?'

" In the end of 1854 it pleased God to bring home with power to my heart, that it would profit me nothing if I gained the whole world and lost my own soul." It was, he goes on to tell us, one evening, at the beginning of November, when this realization first broke in upon him. He was sitting playing cards in the house he had rented for the shooting season on Dallas moors in Morayshire, when suddenly he was seized with a sensation of illness and an impression that he was about to die. " I said to my son, ' I am a dead man! take me upstairs.' As soon as this was done I threw myself down on the bed. My first thought then was: Now, what will my forty-four years of following the devices of my own heart profit me? In a few minutes I shall be in hell, and what good will all these things do me, for which I have sold my soul?"

From that moment, though his illness soon passed, Brownlow North was a changed man. His outlook was changed; now the Being of God, the immortality of the soul, and salvation through Christ alone, became great realities to him. His habits changed; now he learned what it was to pray and to love the Word of God. His purpose in life changed; he lived no more to please himself but to serve his Creator and Redeemer. In short, Brownlow North experienced what everyone experiences who becomes a Christian; he had, in the words of Scripture, been " born again " and passed from death unto life. Indeed, not only did Brownlow North become a Christian, but like the Apostle Paul of old, he became a preacher of the Gospel, which he had so long neglected.

It was five years later, in the summer of 1859, that we found Brownlow North crossing to Ireland. The passing of a hundred years can dim the memory of even the most arresting events and there are probably few today who remember the significance of the year

1859. It was a year which the Christian church has cause to remember to the end of time. A great spiritual awakening had broken upon this land. Men and women who had had no concern about their souls in all their lives, suddenly became aware that they were sinners needing salvation; church-goers who had sat thoughtlessly for years listening to sermons, suddenly awoke to the realities of an eternal world; ministers began to preach with a new authority; factory workers carried Bibles to their benches; public houses closed and began a new trade of selling religious books. In short, the Spirit of God was working upon the hearts of men, and nowhere was this more evident than in Northern Ireland.

While there were many who were staggered by such events as these, they were not strange to Brownlow North. He knew what it was suddenly to be arrested by a Divine hand and he knew personally the reality of the concern which multitudes were then experiencing. It was thus natural that ministers in Ireland—thronged with hearers—should turn to Brownlow North for help, and it was in response to their earnest invitations that he preached incessantly throughout the length and breadth of Ulster during July and August, 1859. The amazing scenes of those months are more than can be described in a few lines; a full account of them will be found in such books as William Gibson's *Year of Grace*. Suffice it to say that churches were far too small for the hearers. There was an intense hunger to hear the Word of God. Open-air services became a common thing and we find Brownlow North addressing congregations of some 4,000 to 5,000 in the market place at Londonderry, 7,000 at Portrush, 11,000 at Ballymena and 12,000 at Newtonlimavady!

It is important to realise that the contents of this book were originally prepared in these circumstances, and preached during the revival of 1859. These chapters were not composed in the isolation of a study —remote from the affairs of life and the everyday needs of men and women—rather they were composed to help just such people as ourselves.

Could we summon those teeming thousands of a hundred years ago back from their graves, with what astonishment would they review the present indifference of men to the Gospel of Christ! Our land needs that Gospel every bit as desperately as it did in the days of Brownlow North. On all sides there are facts to remind us that life is short, that this present world will not always be our home, "that there is none righteous, no not one," yet how few have any thought for the eternal world that lies before·us! We are all, by nature, like the author of this book was before that momentous night on Dallas moors or like "the Rich Man" was long ago. If this book finds you in that condition, thank God for bringing it into your hands and pray that its message may lead you, as it has led countless others, to a new life and a new world—a life of fellowship with Christ and a world which will abide when this world is no more!

The Publishers,
August, 1960.

CHAPTER I

Earthly Suffering not Salvation

LUKE XVI, 19-31

"THERE was a certain rich man, which was clothed in purple and fine linen, and fared sumptuously every day: and there was a certain beggar named Lazarus, which was laid at his gate, full of sores, and desiring to be fed with the crumbs which fell from the rich man's table: moreover the dogs came and licked his sores. And it came to pass that the beggar died, and was carried by the angels into Abraham's bosom: the rich man also died, and was buried; and in hell he lift up his eyes, being in torments, and seeth Abraham afar off, and Lazarus in his bosom. And he cried and said, Father Abraham, have mercy on me, and send Lazarus, that he may dip the tip of his finger in water, and cool my tongue; for I am tormented in this flame. But Abraham said, Son, remember that thou in thy lifetime receivedst thy good things, and likewise Lazarus evil things: but now he is comforted, and thou art tormented. And beside all this, between us and you there is a great gulf fixed: so that they which would pass from hence to you cannot; neither can they pass to us, that would come from thence. Then he said, I pray thee therefore, father, that thou wouldest send him to my father's house: for I have five brethren; that he may testify unto them, lest they also come into this place of torment. Abraham saith unto him, They have Moses and the prophets; let them hear them. And he said, Nay, father Abraham: but if one went unto them from the dead, they will repent. And he said unto him, If they hear not Moses and the prophets, neither will they be persuaded, though one rose from the dead."

Such is the history given us by our Lord Himself of these two men: the Rich Man and Lazarus. I say history, for I am inclined to think it is a history, and not a parable. Jesus introduces it with the words " *There was.*" *There was* a certain rich man, and *there was* a certain beggar. Be it history or parable, however, the lessons taught us are the same; and may God the Holy Spirit, for Jesus Christ's great name's sake, enable me to point them out, and you, oh reader, to receive and profit by them.

There was a certain rich man, and there was a certain beggar. The rich man died, and was lost; the beggar died, and went to heaven: or, to use, as our Lord did, a Jewish expression for the same thing, " was carried by the angels into Abraham's bosom." Now the question that concerns us is evidently this: Why was the rich man lost, and why was the poor man saved? There was nothing in the position of either that would of necessity open or shut to them the gates of heaven. No man was ever lost simply because he was rich, neither was any man ever saved simply because in this world he had been poor and miserable. Both the rich man and the beggar had passed through life in the position in which it had pleased God to place them, and that position could not be in itself a position of sin; on the contrary, to both were entrusted talents which they were bound to employ for God's service, and to both He had given opportunities to honour and to glorify Him. It was not the difference in their earthly position, but the difference in the way in which each improved that position, that made the difference between them when their position was fixed for ever.

And how great, how terrible was that difference! Nothing less than the difference between heaven and hell! A difference differing from all earthly differences, in as much as it is a difference not for time, but for eternity. Doubtless in their earthly positions great was the difference between the Rich Man and Lazarus. The cups of both were full to the brim: the one with almost every good thing, the other with almost every earthly evil; still the very fact that the difference was earthly, robbed it of its substance. The things that are seen are temporal. Life soon passes, and when passed, neither its joys nor its sorrows have any further power. But the things which are not seen are eternal. Once enter on the world that is before you, and be it for joy or sorrow, your position is fixed for ever. The great question for us is not, what is our position, but, are we endeavouring to glorify God in the position in which He has placed us. No matter what it is, it is the one He has chosen for us. It may be above or below the average, but above or below, it has its own privileges and responsibilities; and the day is coming when we must give an account of the way in which we have employed what has been entrusted to us. Think of this.

I will not argue the point as to which of the two, the rich man or the poor, God shows, when He allots him his station in this world, the greatest amount of electing love. Both have their own advantages, which if improved, under the teaching of the Holy Spirit, will lead each alike to Christ and heaven; both have their own peculiar trials and temptations, which, if not watched against, prayed against, striven against, will destroy the souls of each alike. It is possible for the mightiest, the wealthiest, the noblest to glorify God on the earth, to die, and go to heaven; it is possible for the most miserable and afflicted beggar to dishonour God on the earth, to die, and not go to heaven.

I wish this truth was better understood both amongst rich and poor. Being constantly engaged in public speaking, I have neither time nor strength to visit as much as many do amongst any class in private; but even in my small experience of dealing with individuals, I have met instances of the rich pleading their station as an excuse for their irreligion, and the poor their position as a set-off against their sins; the one declaring that, situated as they were, it was impossible for them to come out from the world, and live Christian lives, and consequently of course that it was impossible for them to be saved; and the other, believing that because they had been poor and needy in this world, they could not be poor and needy in the next, and consequently of course that it was impossible for them to be lost.

I propose, God helping me, to speak more fully about the rich presently, therefore will say no more about them just now; but I cannot refrain from mentioning two instances that have come under my own personal observation amongst the poor, where the fullest assurance of salvation was based on the grossest and most soul-destroying ignorance.

I was walking one day in the neighbourhood of Stirling, when a beggar accosted me, and asked an alms. He was an elderly man, and looked very wretched and miserable. I entered into conversation with him, and by degrees began to speak to him about his soul. So far as I could judge, no heathen could be in greater darkness. He seemed to understand nothing of the way of salvation. The name of Jesus Christ he had heard of, but he hardly knew in what connection: certainly the farthest idea from his mind was that He was God manifest in the flesh, dying for such as he was.

I felt somehow at the time a more than usual interest in this man, and being very desirous to awaken in him an anxiety about his future, after some preliminary conversation, said, " To look at you, my friend, I should not think you have had much enjoyment in your past life : nor should I think your time here will be much longer. You know something of what is meant by sorrow and suffering; would you not wish to have done with it when you have done with this world?"

The man's face lighted up with hope and brightness, as he replied,—" Yes, sir; and the thought that I shall then have done with it, is my only happiness on earth. My one pleasure is to know that I must soon die, and that with my life my sorrows and my sufferings will be ended."

" But when you die," I said, " your sorrows and your sufferings will not be ended, if you do not learn now, before you die, to know and to believe in the Lord Jesus Christ. If you die without an interest in Christ, no matter what you may have been here, you will not be saved—you will not go to heaven; and if when you die you do not go to heaven, all the sorrow and suffering you have ever known, will be as nothing compared to your misery for ever and ever."

The man looked at me with perfect incredulity, but the bright smile was still upon his countenance. " No, sir," he said, " you must be wrong there. I do not say that I know Jesus Christ, who you talk so much about; but I know that there are two parties, the rich and the poor, in this world, and that God gives to the rich a good portion here, while to such as me He gives sorrow and suffering. You said just now that you thought I had not had much happiness in this world, and you said right. I have heard of such a thing, but that is all I know about happiness. But when I die my troubles will be all over, and my turn will come. I never will believe that the Almighty would let a person go through the wretchedness and misery that I have suffered here, if He did not intend to make it up to him in the world to come. I have no comfort, no hope on earth but this, that the end of my life will be the end of my troubles."

Poor man! I could do nothing for him. I talked to him for some time, and prayed in my heart for him; but it seemed all in vain: nothing I could say seemed to make the least impression. I can only hope that his eyes have been since opened, but he left me apparently in the full assurance of faith, that though he knew nothing of Jesus Christ, he was going to heaven because he had been a great sufferer, and had a hard lot in this world.

The other was even a more painful case. I was asked to go and visit four old women, who lived together in a small apartment provided by the parish, and who were too infirm to attend any place of worship. On going, I found that three were bed-ridden, while the fourth, herself little better, received a trifle from the parish for cooking their food and waiting on the bed-ridden three. It was a sad scene of misery and destitution. Of the three confined to bed, one they told me the doctor said was dying; and though her voice was full and powerful, and her strength, when she aroused herself, far from exhausted, yet the doctor spoke truly, for she died about ten days after I first saw her.

On hearing that she had not long to live, I went over to her bed, and entered into conversation with her; and I must confess that she exceedingly refreshed and delighted me. She knew that she was dying, and talked of it with the greatest joy. So far from terror, she looked forward to it with impatience, speaking of it as the gate to heaven, where there would be no more pain nor sorrow. I cannot say whether or not she mentioned the name of Christ; my impression is she did, for I afterwards found she knew several set phrases and Scripture sentences, which she was in the habit of quoting; but be that as it may, her whole tone and manner was so full of peace and assurance, and *that* in the known prospect of immediate death, that I fancied nothing but Christ could have given it, and she completely deceived me. I went away from her assured of her salvation, and when I thanked God for what He had done for her, it was with a deep feeling that I wished I could change places with her. As I left the room, the old nurse followed me to the door, and thanking me for calling, hoped I would soon come back again. I said I would, and then added what a privilege it was to witness such a death-bed as that of the old woman's inside.

Imagine my astonishment when she told me that that woman was one of the most hardened and unbelieving sinners she had ever known or heard of; it was quite true she was dying, and that she said and very likely believed she was going to heaven; but that while she maintained this, she made the little room in which they all lived a hell. Whole nights would she keep them awake with oaths and cursing. When she was in pain, or if anything displeased her, her passion and the

language in which she gave vent to it, were alike frightful: indeed she thought it well for the rest of them that
she was bed-ridden, for if she had the power she believed that long since in one of her rages she would
have got up and killed them all.

I was perfectly amazed, and went back the next day.
Addressing this dying woman, after I had spoken a few
words to the others, I asked her: " Are you as happy,
and as prepared to die, as you were yesterday?"

" Oh yes," she said: " I am always ready. I wish I
was gone."

" Then you feel quite sure that Christ loves you,"
I said, " and you know that you love Him: you know
that His blood has washed away your sins, and that He
is *your* Saviour?"

" Oh," she said, " some good ladies have been here
talking to me about that; but that is not why I want to
die. I want to die because I have had all my suffering in this world, and so when I die I shall go to
heaven."

" What do you mean?" I asked, horrified.

" I mean," she said, getting angry and speaking
excitedly, as she saw that I did not agree with her; " I
mean that people are never poor and miserable in both
worlds. I have been a poor wretched creature, suffering ill-health and poverty all my days. I have never
known anything but misery; and now I am dying as I
have lived. Do you think God will let me be miserable
in the next world?"

" Woman," I said, " your condition is terrible. You

21

say true when you say your are dying, and you say true when you say you are poor and miserable; but your greatest misery is that you think you are going to heaven when you are going to hell. The Bible says (Acts iv. 12), that there is no other name but the name of Jesus given amongst men whereby we must be saved; and you are not trusting in that Name, but in your own past sorrows and sufferings. God will forgive no man's sins for the sake of what he has suffered here; and as sure as His Word is true, your sufferings in the world you are going into will be greater than any you have ever known, unless you at once give up all dependence on them, and place your hopes on the merits and atonement of Jesus."

Of course I condense the conversation, but after prayer with her and for her, I endeavoured earnestly and affectionately to point her to Christ.

It was with manifest impatience the poor creature even listened to me. "Nonsense," she said: "I again tell you I have had all my suffering here. It is the rich: those who have had a life of pleasure and enjoyment here, and not the poor who will suffer in the world to come."

"It is most true," I said, "that those who have spent their riches in mere earthly pleasure and enjoyment, will most certainly leave it all behind them when they die, and will never know a single moment of pleasure or enjoyment again; but the poor as well as the rich will go to the same place when they die, if they die without Christ. Neither poverty, nor riches, nor prosperity, nor adversity, can in themselves either destroy or save a soul. If the rich man dies in Christ, he will go to heaven: if the poor man dies out of Christ, he will go to hell."

"No, he won't!" she cried, interrupting me: "No, he won't! I'm no scholar, but I know he won't. Its the likes of me that goes to heaven, its the likes of you that goes to hell. I've had all my suffering here, and when I die I shall have no more to suffer; after that I shall always be happy."

It was useless to reason with her, it seemed only to provoke evil temper, and that sometimes to such an extent that I feared she would break out even before me into bad language. I went two or three times to see her, but our interviews were all alike. She was quite happy, she said, if people would only let her alone. She had had all her troubles in this world.

On calling one day I found she had died in the night. Her last words were a mixture,—expressions of rage because something had not been done as she liked, and expressions of delight because she was getting away from them all!

I trust such instances are rare in this Christian country, but I am not sure of it; and even if this particular form of deception is uncommon, it is only one of a legion, with which Satan deceives souls. "Other foundation," says the Apostle, "can no man lay than that is laid, which is Jesus Christ." (1 Cor. iii. 11.) Yet are there not many not on this Foundation who die what is called happily,—die happily without Christ,—

die happily, having no better foundation for their death-bed happiness than had this poor wretched woman.

Of course I do not profess that these conversations are given verbatim, but what I have written gives their sum and substance.

CHAPTER II

How the Beggar became Rich

"THERE was a certain beggar. And it came to pass that the beggar died, and was carried by the angels into Abraham's bosom."

" The beggar died." Blessed moment for the beggar. Conducted by ministering spirits into the presence of the King of kings, God Himself wiped away all tears from his eyes; and amidst the songs of angels and archangels, and the innumerable company before the throne, he who on earth had neither food nor raiment, nor house wherein to lay his head, was welcomed an heir of God, a joint-heir with Christ, and for ever installed in an inheritance in the kingdom of heaven. Oh, the joy of that moment to Lazarus! His last enemy had been destroyed, and death had been to him the gate into everlasting life. His light affliction, which was but for a moment, had worked for him a far more exceeding and eternal weight of glory.

But why was all this? Why was it that when Lazarus died he went to heaven? Was his earthly sorrow and suffering the meritorious and procuring cause? Oh, no: no! Many have suffered as much, and more than ever Lazarus suffered, who have not gone to heaven when they died. Affliction in itself, as we have said before, never could and never did take any one to heaven.

Affliction is a talent. It is true it is a rod: a rod in the hands of a loving Father, which He often uses for His children's good; but it is also a talent,—a talent entrusted to us by God, which He expects us to improve to His glory and to our own everlasting good. If we so improve it, there are few of His gifts for which we shall ultimately more praise Him; for great is the gift with which God entrusts a man, when He entrusts him with affliction. Those that are exercised thereby, and in whom it produces the peaceable fruits of righteousness, will for ever bless Him that sent it, saying " It is good for me that I was afflicted."

But woe to the man who does not see and acknowledge the hand of God in affliction. If it does not soften it hardens, and great, yea deadly is the hardness it produces. Many are there to whom God has sent line upon line, precept upon precept; sorrow, sickness, trial, want, bereavement—evils upon evils, each following each in quick succession, or perhaps coming altogether, and remaining with little variation for months and years, upon whom these things have produced no spiritual impression: under it all, their hearts have remained unhumbled, and their god the god of this world. Awful is the truth, that men may be brought, and many have been brought after years of chastening, to their last days on earth, without ever having been awakened to the least concern about their souls. People whose hearts, like Pharaoh's, in spite of all God's judgments have retained to the last their natural ignorance and their natural enmity, and who have gone out of the world to give an account of the talents that had been entrusted to them, to find that their unsanctified affliction in time had only increased their condemnation for eternity.

But this was not the case with Lazarus. It is true that his afflictions did not take him to heaven, but they taught him that in the things of this world it was useless for him to seek happiness. His worldly portion was affliction, and not contented with that, he sought and found another portion; that portion did what no earthly portion ever yet did for any man : *it satisfied him.* Satisfied him in the midst of all his trials while he lived, satisfied him in death, satisfied him when his eternal state was decided, is satisfying him now, and will satisfy him, and that increasingly, for ever and ever. Lazarus being unsatisfied, and feeling that things temporal could never satisfy him, fled for refuge to things spiritual. He went to the Scriptures and the God of the Scriptures; and found in the Scriptures, under God's teaching, a satisfying portion : he found JESUS CHRIST.

From that moment, the beggar in his rags with Christ for his portion, was happier at the Rich Man's gate every day, than the Rich Man with purple, and fine linen, and sumptuous fare for his portion every day. The Rich Man could never say more than that he had a portion "in things present"; but Lazarus, from the moment he found Christ, could apply to himself what Paul said to the Corinthians: "all things are yours: the world, or life, or death, or things present, or things to come; all are yours and ye are Christ's; and Christ is God's." (1 Cor. iii. 21-23.) And at last it came to pass that the beggar died, and He who had been his portion in life was his portion in death. It was because he had sought and found Christ, and for that reason only, that when the beggar died he was carried by the angels into Abraham's bosom.

Some may ask by what authority I say all this. I answer, on the very highest and most unquestionable, even on the authority of the Word of God. If you deny the authority of that Word, then we have no common basis on which we can meet together; but if you admit that God's Word is truth, then you must admit that no man goeth unto the Father but by Christ; then you must admit that there is no other name, save the name of Jesus, given amongst men, whereby we can be saved. Now Lazarus went to the Father, *therefore he must have gone by Christ*; Lazarus was saved, *therefore he must have been saved by Christ.*

Anything may take a man to Christ. A rich man may feel as Solomon felt: that this world can be no satisfying portion, and the thought may take him to Christ. A poor man may feel as Lazarus felt: that this world can be no satisfying portion, and the thought may take him to Christ. Prosperity, adversity, health, sickness, joy, sorrow, the fall of a leaf, or the flight of a bird,—anything, everything, no matter what, may be made effectual to this end, in the hands of God the Spirit. There is nothing that may not take a man to Christ, but *there is nothing but Christ can take a man to heaven.*

It must have been a great privilege to have conversed with this poor beggar as he lay at the Rich Man's gate. It is true he did not live in times of such clear Gospel light as we do, yet I think it likely his love, joy, peace, long-suffering, gentleness, goodness, faith, meekness, charity, were manifest to all who knew him, and would have put to shame much of what is now called Christianity. I am quite sure that he firmly believed in himself as the chief of sinners, and that the BLOOD OF ATONEMENT was his only hope. Abraham rejoiced to see Christ's day; and he saw it, and was glad; Moses wrote of Him, and David called Him " Lord "; and under the guidance of the same Spirit that taught Abraham, Moses, and David, Lazarus knew Christ, believed in Him, and was saved by Him.

Reader, has the Holy Spirit taught you to know Christ? There is a knowledge that " puffeth up," but this is not the knowledge of those that are taught of God. If you know Christ by the teaching of the Holy Spirit, you love Him, and if you love Him you try to serve Him, and promote His glory. This is the knowledge that profiteth. If you have it, thank God with your whole heart, for it is He alone to whom is due all the glory,—it is He alone who has made you to differ. If you have it not, and die without it, no matter what may have been your earthly circumstances, your eternal portion will not be with Abraham and Lazarus.

But not only did the beggar die, but we read, " the Rich Man also died."

What! Did it happen then to the Rich Man even as it happened to the poor? Could neither wealth, rank, influence, nor position procure for this man that he should not have died? No! These things could procure him many luxuries, and save him while on earth from many disagreeables, but *they could not purchase life*; there is no man, saith God, that hath power over the Spirit to retain the Spirit, neither hath he power in the day of death; there is no discharge in that war. He who tells us, " It came to pass that Lazarus died," tells us, " the Rich Man also died."

Satan, if he possibly can hinder it, will never let a man remember that he must die; consequently it is one of the marks of Satan's people that they forget death; and forgetting death, they forget God and judgment, and speak and act as if their life on earth was everlasting. Nevertheless, dear reader, unless the Lord Jesus comes first, you, whoever you are, will one day certainly die. That day may look far off now, and so it did once to the Rich Man. In the days of his youth, in the pride of health and strength, when clothed in purple and fine linen, and surrounded by sumptuous fare and pleasant company—courted, feted, praised, flattered, and perhaps loved,—oh, if anyone in such times ever spoke to him about death, how distant, how dreamy and unsubstantial death appeared! how unnecessary the subject, how out of place and unwelcome. But for all that death came. Forget it as he might, even in his youngest and merriest days it was always creeping closer to him; every night as he lay down he had a day less to live; death was a day nearer to him than it was in the morning; and at last, slowly and imperceptibly, but still at last, the day which had once seemed so far off, arrived, and death *did* come. One morning the sun arose on the last day of the purple and fine linen and sumptuous fare; and as it happened to the beggar so it also happened to the Rich Man: "*the Rich Man also died.*"

And as it happened to the beggar, and as it happened to the Rich Man, so I say again, it will also happen to you. It may be to-day, or it may not be for years, but sooner or later, as men said of them, so will they one day be saying of you: HE IS DEAD.

HE IS DEAD! How often have you said it of others? You have said it of young as well as of old; of the apparently healthy as well as of the infirm and sick; of those not only that you thought likely to die, but of those you thought must unlikely; of those you thought as little likely to die as you do yourself this minute. These all died when you did not expect it: and so, when you do not expect it, perhaps will you; at all events, you will die. "It is appointed unto all men once to die." As you have so often said of others, so will others one day be saying of you: HE IS DEAD! May God the Holy Spirit bless this thought to you, for it is a solemn one.

And what makes this thought of death,—or rather, what should make this thought of death so solemn? I have just quoted from Heb. ix. 27, "It is appointed unto all men once to die." Do you remember the word of God which follows? It is the word that follows which makes death so solemn. "It is appointed unto all men once to die, but *after this the judgment.*" Two certainties: first death, and after death the final, irrevocable judgment. That they might escape this judgment, good would it be for some men if they could die like the beasts; but that cannot be. Once born, man must go on to death, and judgment. This corruptible must put on incorruption, and this mortal must put on immortality. Once born, the existence of man becomes as everlasting as the existence of God; and let him employ as he may the time given him on earth, on earth it is appointed to him to live a certain period; then it is appointed to him to die: and after this THE JUDGMENT.

Something more than mad are they who do not know and consider the value of time. I would ask anyone who believes the Bible to observe how multitudes use time, and then to say whether such multitudes are not madder than madmen. What is the length of every man's life REALLY? Everlasting. What is the length of his life on earth? At the longest, some seventy or eighty years. The first seventy or eighty years then of an existence that is everlasting is all that is allotted to man in which to prepare for his eternal future. Should not this fact, for which the truth of God is pledged, arrest indifference, and make the most thoughtless think? Should it not bring us all into close dealing with ourselves, as to how and for what we are spending time? Jesus Christ, the " Wisdom of God," says, " Lay up for yourselves treasures in heaven"; Jesus Christ, "the Truth," says, Every man is a fool who layeth up treasure for himself, and is not RICH towards God. And may not even the simplest understand that that man must be under some strong delusion, who, professing to believe that he is immortal, lives only, or even primarily, for the things of earth? What were his purple and fine linen and sumptuous fare to the Rich Man, when his doctor told him he must die? And what will it be to you in that same hour, if you have gained the whole world and lost your own soul?

Oh, who can hope to tell others, or even understand himself, the value of time? Always excepting the unspeakable gift of Christ and His Spirit, God has given to man nothing more valuable. Time is man's *day of salvation*. As long as a man has time, though he is the greatest sinner on earth, he may repent, believe the Gospel, and be saved. As long as a man has time, he who is saved may daily lay up treasure in heaven, growing in grace, and in the knowledge of his Lord and Saviour. There was a servant of Christ's who received from his Lord a pound, and while he had time he made it two pounds. That servant has since entered into the joy of his Lord, and is now ruler over two cities. There was a servant of Christ's who received from his Lord a pound, and while he had time he made it five pounds.

That servant has since entered into the joy of his Lord, and is now ruler over five cities. There was a servant of Christ's who received from his Lord a pound, and while he had time he made it ten pounds. That servant has since entered into the joy of his Lord, and is now ruler over ten cities. There will be those who sit on the right hand and on the left hand side of the Lord Jesus in His kingdom; whoever they are, they will be hell deserving sinners, saved like you and me by grace; but for all that we may be sure that when they had it, no two sinners on earth ever made better use of their time.

Looking at it as man's opportunity, think of what is the value of time; think of what you *may* do with it; think of what you *are* doing with it!

Oh, ye unsaved, eternity is before you! Spend not your time for time. Oh, ye redeemed, eternity is before you! Spend not your time for time. Redeem time for Him who has redeemed you. Every moment you redeem brings glory to God, and is treasure laid up for yourself in heaven; every moment you lose is so much wasted of your Lord's goods, and so much lost to yourself of an eternal weight of glory.

CHAPTER III

How the Rich Man became Poor

THE Beggar died: the Rich Man also died: the Rich Man also died, and was buried. It is not said that the beggar had any funeral. Man paid him no honour; but he had the honour that cometh from God only. The beggar died, and "was carried by the angels into Abraham's bosom."

It is expressly recorded, however, that the rich man was buried. Doubtless the pomp and pageantry of his funeral was all that he would have himself desired, had he been on earth; and all that could gratify the pride of his five surviving brothers: but while the appointed mourners followed the dead body to the ancestral burying-place, and fixed the flattering monument in its prepared place, where, oh where, was the Rich Man himself? Jesus tells us—*He was in hell, in torments.* "The Rich Man also died, and was buried; and in hell he lift up his eyes, being in torments."

Lazarus died: the Rich Man died. So far there was one event to each alike: but "after death, came the judgment"; and how different to each was the event in the judgment that followed? Lazarus died; and, by the

35

judgment of God, went immediately to heaven: the Rich Man died; and, by the judgment of God, went immediately to hell.

As this history is narrated by our Lord Himself, we know that it is pure and unmixed truth. How unanswerably, then, does it confute and overthrow the unscriptural doctrine of purgatory? Let no man deceive you. The teaching of neither Church nor Churchman, is to be believed, if that teaching is contrary to Scripture; and that teaching is contrary to Scripture, which says that by personal, or any other suffering, there can be repentance, or atonement, or salvation, beyond the grave. On this subject, the Word of God is clear: THAT tells us that here on earth, both God and man may repent them of the evil. A wicked man may repent him of the evil he has done against God and his own soul, turn from it, and obtain mercy; and God may repent Him of the evil He has purposed to do against a wicked man, turn from it, and show him mercy: but there is no μετά νοια, no change of mind, no repentance in the grave. Let it once be truly said of a man, HE IS DEAD, and the teaching of the Bible is, that neither in God's heart nor his own can there ever again be any place found for repentance. As it was with the Rich Man and Lazarus so will it be with us all. Immediately after death our portions will be fixed: fixed in heaven or in hell, unchangeably, and for ever.

Do not forget what I said in the last chapter about the value of time.

How the Rich Man became Poor

And now, seeing that we have arrived at this truth, —the Rich Man was lost; there arises the all important question, What was his sin? That it was soul-destroying, is quite clear; for it barred heaven against him, and sank him in everlasting ruin: but what was it? We have before shown that as the poverty of Lazarus was not his righteousness, so the riches of the Rich Man were not his sin. It is no sin to be rich. Abraham, called in Scripture "The Friend of God" (2 Chron. xx. 7), was rich; and David, Solomon, Joseph, and many others, were "clothed in purple and fine linen, and fared sumptuously every day": yet these were all saved when they died, and so have been multitudes of others like them. It was not the position in which God had placed him that kept the Rich Man out of heaven: that gave him advantages above most, both for glorifying God, and laying up for himself spiritual treasure; and, doubtless, the unemployed advantages of that position increased his guilt and condemnation: but his position was not his sin. What, then, was the sin of the Rich Man?

To answer the question, What was the sin of the Rich Man? has been the chief reason for which I have written this little book. Oh, that God would enable me to expose it, and bring it home, by the power of the Holy Ghost, to every heart and conscience! I believe it to be THE SIN which has been the great and foundational cause of the destruction of every man who has perished since the promise was given,—"The seed of the woman shall bruise the serpent's head." I believe it to be THE SIN which, from the date of that promise to this present day, has kept the world lying in wickedness: THE SIN that is sending, not rich men only, but high and low, rich and poor,—the moral and respectable, no less than the openly profligate and godless,—every class and section of the human race,—excepting only those who have been born again of the Spirit,—to join, when they leave this world, the Rich Man in his place of torment.

Let no one think it was a sin that a poor man cannot commit. As the Rich Man could have sought and found what Lazarus sought, and have been saved; so Lazarus could have sinned, as the Rich Man sinned, and have perished for ever.

What was it? Before we can answer the question, we must ask another. What was, by nature, the real condition of the Rich Man? In what was his lot like, and in what was it unlike, the generality of his fellow creatures?

First, in what was his lot unlike? It was unlike, in almost every earthly circumstance. Few are born to purple and fine linen and sumptuous fare every day. Few, comparatively, are placed as he was, in such a position of ease and affluence, as to enable them to command at will, all the " good things " of this world. When man ate of the forbidden tree, and sinned, God said to him, " Cursed be the ground, for thy sake: in the sweat of thy face, shalt thou eat thy bread." But this curse, so keenly felt by almost all, seemed to have fallen harmlessly on the Rich Man. He never experienced, and perhaps never even knew, that there was a curse upon the earth; a curse not only upon the earth, but upon himself personally, in common with his fellow men. His own idea was that he had nothing in common with his fellow men. He was the impersonation, the exact type of him who stumbled Asaph the Psalmist, and whose description he gives us in the seventy-third Psalm. First, says the Psalmist, " My feet were almost gone; my steps had well nigh slipped ": and then he tells us why,—" For I was envious at the foolish, when I saw the prosperity of the wicked ": " they are not in trouble as other men; neither are they plagued like other men ": " they prosper in the world ": " increase in riches ": " have more than heart could wish." This was the picture of the rich man : his position such that the world, seeing nothing left for him to desire, called him blessed; and even God's people, unless kept by grace, found their corruptions stirred, and envy rising in them when they looked upon his prosperity. In so far as all this went his lot was unlike the generality of his fellow creatures.

But was the lot of the Rich Man so cast that he had escaped all evil ? Had he no need to be supplied, and no want that he shared in common with the rest of the sons of men ? Alas, yes ! though it is probable while on earth he never knew it, and certainly never felt it. He was born with a want,—the greatest of all wants; yet a want without which, whether rich or poor, no child of Adam ever yet was born. The rich man was born into the world heir to purple and fine linen and sumptuous fare, but he was born into the world WITHOUT GOD.

Reader, my last words are solemn truth; but, nevertheless, they are truth. Whatever his other circumstances may be, this is the universal want of every human being. However much we may differ from our fellow men in other respects, in this we are all alike. We are born into the world WITHOUT GOD; and unless between our birth and our grave we are born again of God the Spirit, we live and die without God. In such a case, though we have gained the whole world, good would it have been for us if we had never been born at all.

St. Paul, in writing to the converts he had made at Ephesus, describes to them, in ch. ii. 12, what they were before they were converted; and when he described them, he described the whole world by nature. " At that time,"—that is before God quickened you (see first verse of chapter),—" At that time, ye were without Christ, being aliens from the commonwealth of Israel, and strangers from the covenants of promise, having no hope, and without God in the world." Now this little verse, which expresses in substance all that language can express of human want and woe, may be condensed, and summed up in the two words with which it ends: " WITHOUT GOD." He who has not God has not Christ, and he who has not Christ is an alien and a stranger to all true good; if he has any hope for the future, it is unscriptural and soul-deceiving, for as sure as he dies without God, he will perish, as did the Rich Man.

I have said that all that can be said of earthly want and woe is summed up in the two words, " WITHOUT GOD "; and I have also said that all men are WITHOUT GOD by nature. Now both statements are true in their very plainest and fullest senses; and he who has not sought and found God since he was born, no matter what may be the prosperity of his worldly circumstances, is a far more miserable and pitiable object than ever was Lazarus at the Rich Man's gate.

When God placed Adam in the Garden of Eden, He " commanded the man, saying, Of every tree in the garden thou mayest freely eat, but of the tree of the knowledge of good and evil, thou shalt not eat of it : for in the day that thou eatest thereof, thou shalt surely die." Adam, the man, did eat : and in that day, according to God's Word,—yea in that hour, in that moment, while the flavour of the forbidden fruit was yet fresh upon his palate,—he died. His body did not die that minute : Adam lived many hundred years after his sin : but in the instant that he broke God's commandment he lost, not temporal, but eternal life, and Adam's soul died.

God is the Life of the soul. No soul is alive that has not God; and in the same moment that he sinned, *God left Adam.* That Eternal Life which came into the world with him, returned into the bosom of the Father; and with a body still able to perform all the uses and functions of natural life, Adam became spiritually dead. In the moment that he sinned, Adam was " *without God in the world.*"

This is the death that Adam died in Paradise; this is

the death that, in consequence of their descent from him, every child of Adam has died (all born into the world without God); this is the death that the Lord Jesus Christ, when He came to redeem us from death, died for us, and which wrung from Him the agonizing cry, "My God, my God, why hast Thou forsaken Me!"

Let who may argue to the contrary,—to be without God is death; and not only is it death, but there is no other death. To him who has God, the death of the body is not really death,—it is spoken of in Scripture as "a falling asleep"; but he who has not God, is dead. He may have a name to live, he may not only join in all the active pursuits and pleasures of the world, but he may be wise in it and prosper in it: he may even perform all the outward duties of religion to the satisfaction of his fellow men, and the delusion of his own soul; yet if he has not God, he is dead. "He that hath the Son," saith the Scripture, "hath life; and he that hath not the Son of God, hath not life." And, amongst other reasons, this is true because the Father and the Son are One: so that he that hath not the Son hath not the Father, and consequently hath not life, because he is "without God in the world."

When Lazarus and the Rich Man were born, both were born "without Christ" and "without God." When Lazarus and the Rich Man died, Lazarus had God and the Rich Man had not. Lazarus when on earth was discontented without God, and did what the Rich Man might have done had he also been discontented: he sought and found the Lord Jesus Christ. But the Rich

Man felt no need; he had that which satisfied him—purple and fine linen and sumptuous fare; and he felt no desire for the only thing he had not. The Rich Man had everything but God, the beggar had nothing but God, and each was contented with his portion. Lazarus had God, and was contented; the Rich Man was contented without God.

And now, dear reader, do you understand what was the sin of the Rich Man? the sin for which he has been already eighteen hundred years in torment, and which even eternal punishment can never expiate. The sin of the Rich Man was CONTENTMENT WITHOUT GOD. Born without God,—that was his curse; contentment without God,—that was his sin. Was I wrong when I said it was a sin that rich and poor may alike commit? Oh, let rich and poor alike take care, for God is no respecter of persons! Godliness with contentment is great gain, but CONTENTMENT WITHOUT GOD IS DAMNING.

Oh, ye that are contented without God in the world, God's greatest curse on this side of the grave is on you! If you are without God, who is it that reigns in you? Satan: the next strongest power to God, "the prince of the power of the air, the spirit that now worketh in the children of disobedience." (Eph. ii. 2.) Indeed, indeed the statement is not too strong,—that if you are without God and contented, no demoniac in the days of our Lord was ever more completely in the possession of the devil. You doubt this: you boast yourself of your free-agency, and say that you could turn to God easily if you chose; that perhaps you will some day, but that at present you like sin better. You who believe you can give up sin and turn to God when you please, are under a strong delusion to believe a lie. You may be able to do any earthly thing at your own will; you can give your time and thoughts, your money and your best energies, to any of the things of the world that interest you; but you cannot turn from sin, and seek and find God when you please. It is true that if you seek Him He will be found of you, for He has said, " Seek, and you shall find "; but the devil will not even let you seek Him, unless, although unknown to yourself, God is already with you, helping you. Cry to Him to help you : you cannot help yourself without Him. You have only to make the experiment to prove the truth of what I say. You can do anything else you like, because in other difficulties you have only to wrestle against flesh and blood; Satan is indifferent to other things, and makes no opposition. But get anxious about your soul, and try to be a Christian; try to honour God, and keep His commandments; try to live as in your better moments you wish you did, and as you will wish you had when you come to die; try even to put yourself on your knees in the name of Christ, and pray to Him; or to think for ten minutes without distraction of what it is to be without God,—and you will at once prove to yourself that you are wrestling not only against flesh and blood, but against principalities and powers and the rulers of the darkness of this world; and not only wrestling, but utterly powerless in their power. Perhaps you have already tried : many have. Many have

felt at times that it was worse than folly to live only for
this world: that they would like to be, and have set
about trying to be, Christians; but the trial has been a
failure, and their goodness like the early cloud and the
morning dew. Why? Because a strong man kept
them: a stronger than they. They would have liked
to have been, and tried to be, Christians; but Satan did
not like it, and tried to hinder it. What happened? As
they were not so strong as he was, it ended in their
doing not what they wished, but what he wished. Their
wills were overcome, and his will was done: the proof
being they are not now Christians.

Once more then I say, that while by resolution and
natural powers almost any earthly thing may be accomplished, resolution and natural powers are powerless in
spiritual things; that let him boast of his free-agency as
he may, the man who is without God cannot in the
things of God do as he would, but is led captive by
Satan *at his will*. No man by nature can be a Christian,
because by nature man is without God.

Reader, let me ask you in all love, Do you really
believe that in God's sight you are a Christian, or, in
other words, that you have got God? The question is
not, are you moral and respectable,—a good father,
mother, husband, wife, child, friend, neighbour; it is
not, are you true and just in your dealings, or, do you
attend strictly to all the church duties of your religious
denomination. Many do this, and are all and more than
I have named, and yet are not Christians,—not saved,—
because they have not got God. The one question is,

Have you got God? If you have, you have received Him since you were born, for be you who or what you may, when you came into the world God was not in you. Those who have got God have experienced a second birth, they have been born again of the Spirit; the Holy Ghost has come upon them, and Christ has been formed in them, and by the Spirit that dwelleth in them they have been made the temples of God. The object of Christ's work on earth was not only to make a way by which man could approach God, but by which, as a God of mercy, God could get access to man. It was man's sin that put the barrier between himself and God, and to remove that barrier Christ died. Christ shed His blood to satisfy the claims of God's justice against man : and so, putting away sin by the sacrifice of Himself, made a way by which God could return to man. God left Adam because he sinned, and thus (as to be without God is death) Adam died : God comes back to the child of Adam when he believes in Jesus, and thus (as to have God is life) the child of Adam lives.

Now these truths are absolutely necessary to salvation; without knowing them and receiving them no man can be saved : yet multitudes know nothing of them; and why? Because multitudes are CONTENTED WITHOUT GOD. It is the office of God the Spirit to take of the things that are Jesus Christ's, and show them unto men : and the natural man has not the Spirit of God; for this reason these truths are foolishness to him, so that he cannot know them or receive them. If he had the Holy Spirit he would do both, for when God the

Spirit is come into a man He teacheth him " all things,"
and guideth him into the way of " all truth." A man
can do all things through Christ strengthening him, but
he can do nothing who is WITHOUT GOD. Hath not the
Lord Himself said, " Without Me ye can do nothing "?
(1 Cor. ii. 14; John xiv. 16; xv. 5; xvi. 3; Phil. iv. 13.)

Which was the richer man : the Rich Man, who had
everything but God, or the beggar, who had nothing
but God? To the Rich Man, when on earth, it would
have seemed " foolishness " to have said, " The beggar
with God "; but now, if he could come back and speak
to us, after having felt for eighteen hundred years what
it is to be without God, how do you think *he* would
answer the question?

Deeper than the human heart can fathom is the
meaning of the words WITHOUT GOD; yet, what it is to
be without God is a lesson that either in this world as
Lazarus did, or in the next world as the Rich Man did,
every man must learn, and come to understand for himself. He who learns it here may bless the Lord for it,
for HERE no man need remain a moment without God.
Invitation follows invitation, and promise promise, to
all who are hungering and athirst for Him; indeed it is
hard to conceive of a more blessed state on earth than
the state of that man or woman who is able to cry from
the heart, " My soul is athirst for God." But he who
never thirsts for God here, will thirst for Him before
he has been dead a minute; he who never longs for a
Saviour on earth, will most surely feel his want of a
Saviour in hell. The Rich Man was contented without

God in the world, but as soon as he was in hell he realized his need, and his first cry was, " I thirst."

A frightful place is hell in which for the first time to learn the agony of thirst. It is described in the Bible as " the pit where there is no water." (Zech. ix. 11.) Christ did not go to the angels who fell from their first estate, but to earth, with His plan of mercy; and He brought back the God of mercy, not to devils, but to men. For Christ's sake God will give His Holy Spirit to any man on earth who asks Him; but Christ has not brought back God to devils : there is no Holy Spirit to allay man's cravings, or satisfy his wants, in hell. It is true God is in hell, for God is everywhere; but it is God *out of Christ* : God taking vengeance on those who lived contented without Him in this world : God, a consuming fire! (Psalm cxxxix. 8.)

He who would escape the Rich Man's fate must beware of the Rich Man's sin : CONTENTMENT WITHOUT GOD.

CHAPTER IV

The Poor Rich Man

ALAS, for the poor Rich Man, how many things he does now that he never did on earth. Old things have passed away, all things have become new. The purple, the fine linen, the sumptuous fare, are gone for ever, and in their place there is torment, want, prayer: and, though last mentioned, not the least point recorded for our learning,—the eyes of the Rich Man have been opened, and he sees the kingdom of heaven.

Oh, how terribly it must increase the agony of the people in hell to see the kingdom of heaven! The Rich Man lifts up his eyes, being in torments, and sees Abraham afar off, and Lazarus in his bosom. Until he was in hell the Rich Man had never seen heaven, for he had lived and died without being born again; and, says the Scripture, "Except a man be born again, he cannot see the kingdom of heaven." It is possible that while on earth he may have seen something of the kingdom of hell. I believe most men who live in a Christian country, under certain dispensations of God's providence, at some period or other of their lives get more or less vividly a view of the kingdom of hell. Sickness, the

49

death of a friend or relative, a stirring sermon, a conversation with a faithful Christian,—these and many
other things may bring a man to think about eternity,
and ask himself the question, What is to become of me
when I die? In such cases conscience often gives the
true answer: *You will go to hell.* The thought is
horrible,—more horrible at the moment than the mind
can bear; and dear as are his sins, and great as will be
the sacrifice, he determines to give them all up, and to
live the rest of his days so that when he dies he may
escape hell. In the moment of such convictions he sees
this much of truth, that it will profit a man nothing if
he gains the whole world, and loses his own soul. But
the heart of man was never yet changed from the love
of sin to the love of God by a mere slavish fear of
punishment; and unless it undergoes this change, man
can never enter into the kingdom of heaven. I do not
say despise the fear of hell. The devil never gave a
man even a slavish fear of God; and if you have any
thought at all about eternity, it is of God's mercy, and
may be to you the fear of the Lord, which is the beginning of wisdom. Go to Christ with it, and believe what
He tells you in His Word. If your fear brings you to
Him who has said, " I will in no wise cast out," men
may call it slavish, or by what name they will, but it
will be to you a blessed fear, a fear made instrumental
by God to the saving of your soul. But for all this, such
a view of eternity may be, and too often is, only a carnal
fear, passing away with the circumstances that gave it
birth. A man may see the kingdom of hell in this world,

and forget it; but let a man, his eyes being opened by God's Spirit, once see the kingdom of heaven, and he will never forget it. It may be obscured from his view for a season, but if he once really sees it, he will never permanently lose sight of it. " Eye hath not seen " (that is the natural eye), " nor ear heard, neither hath it entered into the heart of man to conceive the things which God hath prepared for them that love Him "; but to him who sees the kingdom of heaven these things have been revealed by the Spirit of God : who in showing him the kingdom, hath also shown him the King : given him a glimpse not only of the pleasures that are at God's right hand for evermore, but a discovery of God Himself. From that moment, the moment that a man on earth really sees God, nothing less than God can satisfy him; henceforth he counts all things but loss for the excellency of the knowledge of Christ Jesus his Lord. If at any time he does not, it is because for the time he has lost sight of God; for the man who sees the Lord *alway* before him, will not be moved.

The Rich Man lived and died without God, and never on earth saw the kingdom of heaven; but now in hell his eyes have been opened to see. " In torments he lifts up his eyes, and sees Abraham afar off, and Lazarus in his bosom."

Again I say how the sight, adding mental agony to bodily, must have increased the torments of the poor Rich Man. He now sees not only what must for ever be his portion, but what for ever that portion might have been; not only the misery to which he has brought himself, but the glory past knowledge from which he has excluded himself. How literal and real are those things to him now which once seemed so dreamy and unsubstantial. God, Christ, the Holy Spirit, the devil and his angels, are now too convincingly proved to be real persons: heaven and hell real places. And, oh, who can describe the agony with which he realizes to himself, that while there once was a time when he might have sought and found God, and been made meet to be a partaker of an inheritance with the saints, he is now not only doomed to spend eternity with the devil, but for ever shut out from the kingdom of heaven!

But not only does the Rich Man see what he never saw on earth, but his very first act in hell is to do what he never did on earth. No sooner was he in that place of torment than he began to pray. "He cried and said, Father Abraham, have mercy on me, and send Lazarus that he may dip the tip of his finger in water, and cool my tongue, for I am tormented in this flame."

What a lesson have we here! May you to whom God now sends it, profit by it. Do you obey the commandment, "in all things by prayer and supplication to make your requests known unto God"? Do you feel your need, as one born into the world without God, of seeking and finding God? Are you *really* desirous to get your need supplied? Does God know you are desirous, because He constantly hears you in your secret chamber, begging and praying Him to give you His Holy Spirit, which is only another way of saying, give me THYSELF? Are you, in short, a man of prayer? Do you believe it has ever been witnessed of you in heaven as it was of Paul, " Behold he prayeth " ? If not, be quite sure that when you die you will go where the Rich Man went, and that the first thing you will do when you get there will be to pray. Before the Rich Man was in hell five minutes he began to pray. Our Saviour records it as his first act. " He lifted up his eyes and saw "; and the moment he saw, " *he cried, saying.*"

This will always be the case the moment a man for the first time sees the kingdom of heaven. Whether that first time be in heaven or in hell makes no difference; the moment a man sees the kingdom of heaven, he is certain to begin to pray. The reason is this, *he sees a satisfying portion, and his heart thirsts after it.* If this happens in this world, his prayer will be heard, and for Christ's sake, and by Christ, his hungering and thirsting will be satisfied; but if it occurs in hell, the prayer will be too late,—for man's need can only be satisfied by Christ, and there is no Christ in hell.

This cry for water was the first real prayer the Rich Man had ever uttered. He might have " *said his prayers,*" as people call it, night and morning when on earth; but now he was no longer merely saying prayers, but *praying*; the words of his lips were the genuine desires of his heart: he really and truly wanted that for which he professed to ask. Had he so prayed on earth, God would have given him rivers of living water; but he had not so prayed; indeed he could not, for on earth he felt no need of what he wanted in hell. It is possible, I say again, that he might regularly have *said his prayers*, but the Rich Man never *prayed* until he lifted up his eyes in torments; he had nothing to pray for till then : on earth he had everything except God, and on earth he felt no need of God. There can be no real prayer where there is no sense of need.

Would that the vast distinction between saying prayers and praying was more pressed home upon congregations by their ministers, and on the world generally, by godly teachers and other Christians. How comparatively small compared with those who content themselves with what they term *saying their prayers*, is the number of those who really pray. Many have *said their prayers* from their earliest childhood, who have never prayed; many have for years knelt night and morning at the family altar, and joined Sabbath after Sabbath in professed worship, who have never prayed; many, both in public and in private, have put themselves daily from their youth upwards in the attitude of prayer, and uttered from the mouth words of prayer, whose so-called prayers have not only not been prayer, but blasphemy.

SAYING PRAYERS WITHOUT PRAYING IS BLASPHEMY! God has said, " The Lord will not hold him guiltless that taketh His name in vain." Yet I believe that no greater breach of the third commandment ascends from earth into the ears of God, than that which too often ascends from the closet and from family circles, excepting only that which ascends on the Sabbath day from the public assemblies of God's professing worshippers. Who can deny that multitudes of people who have been baptized into the name of Christ, and who would, if you doubted their Christianity, think you yourself were no Christian, go up to their different churches on the Sabbath day for no other reason than that it is the custom : go up expecting to be no better for going up, and totally forgetful that if they are not the better they must be the worse. Multitudes of such have forgotten, and multitudes of such perhaps have never known that the Scripture hath said, if the Word of God is not unto those who hear it a savour of life unto life, it is a savour of death unto death. Yet do not a vast proportion of professing worshippers go up without any realization that they are going up to hear for life or death. Are they solemnized by the recollection, or indeed do many of them even recollect at all that when they pray they are speaking to God, and God hears them; and that when they hear His Word read or preached, God is speaking to them, and expects them to attend and obey ? Do they not rather go up utterly unsolemnized, and enter God's house of prayer, and put themselves in the attitude of prayer, with a heart altogether prayerless ?

In a prayerless spirit men go up to God's house of prayer; in a prayerless spirit they put themselves in the attitude of prayer; and thus in a prayerless spirit invoke God's special attention,—for the attitude of prayer is in itself a prayer, and says as plainly as words could speak it, " Oh, God, let Thine eye rest upon me !"

And God's eye does rest on all who put themselves in the attitude of prayer; from the moment he bows his head to *say his prayers* to the moment in which he leaves the place of worship, God's eye is never off the professing worshipper, and His ear is open, attending to what he says. And what does the eye of God too often see, and His ear too often hear? He sees people, professedly engaged in His worship, not only forgetful, but so absolutely destitute of the fear of God, that they pour forth from their lips a series of supplications for things for which their hearts feel no need; for things for which they have no desire; for things for which, though they profess to ask, they would rather be without; for things which God has offered them again and again, and which they have again and again rejected! Can there be greater blasphemy?

Let me say a little more about this. If uttered, for instance, without desire and without a sense of need, what can more blasphemously break the third commandment than the prayers offered up by members of the Church of England, when using our Liturgy on the Lord's day? And remember that, although I have mentioned the prayers of the Church of England, because I have there got the very letter of the words used, that the prayers of all the Evangelical Churches are the same in substance, expressing the same wants, and professing to seek the same blessings as the petitions used in the English service.

That service begins by calling on the worshippers to fall upon their knees, and confess their sins. Whether they kneel or not, they put themselves in the attitude of prayer, and thus having invoked His attention, they begin to speak to God. Almighty and most merciful

Father, we have erred and strayed from Thy ways. We have offended against Thy holy laws. We have left undone what we should have done, and done what we ought not to have done. There is no health in us. Have mercy upon us, miserable offenders. Spare Thou them which confess their faults. Restore Thou them which are penitent.

This is part of the Confession. Seeing what we see and knowing what we know, can we, with the greatest stretch of charity, believe that the generality of the worshippers feel the reality of what they utter : that they are miserable sinners, that they need to be spared, need to be restored, and are truly penitent? Whether they feel it or not, however, they go on to pray : " Grant, oh, most merciful Father, for Christ's sake, that we may hereafter live a godly, righteous, and sober life, to the glory of Thy holy name."

Now I would ask any man who is willing to take one atom of thought about the matter, whether a person, feeling neither sorrow for past sin nor intention for the future of trying to live a godly, righteous, and sober life, to the glory of God, can commit a more frightful act of blasphemy, than to call upon God to listen to him while he utters the words of this confession and prayer?

Then follows the Lord's Prayer. " Hallowed be Thy name. Thy kingdom come. Thy will be done on earth as it is in heaven." These petitions are poured into the ears of God from every mouth in the congregation; yet how many prove by their everyday life that they desire God's name to be hallowed? How many would truly welcome Him if, in answer to their prayer, Christ's kingdom really was to come? How many would remain to live and reign with Him, if only those were left whose hearts as well as whose lips had prayed, " Thy will be done on earth as it is in heaven." These things will all yet be: God's name will be hallowed, His kingdom will come, and His will will be done on earth as it is in heaven; but when they are, many who have professed to pray for them on earth will begin to pray to the rocks to cover them and the hills to hide them, and, in the end, as the poor Rich Man did, for a drop of water to cool their tongues.

I might go on in this same strain through the whole service of the Church of England, as also through the usual extempore petitions of all the Evangelical congregations; but I will not press the subject further; I have said sufficient, I hope, to make my reader *think*. My desire is to get all to remember that when a person puts himself in the attitude of prayer, he immediately, and by his own act and deed, invites the special attention of God. His position is then a very solemn one, and surely he should be careful what he says; specially should he be careful not to mock God by professing to ask for what He knows he does not want. To utter a string of petitions in which the heart takes no interest is, I again repeat, blasphemy, and not prayer, and they who are guilty of such sin do the devil service, while they provoke and dishonour God.

CHAPTER V

He Prays

THE prayer of the Rich Man,—"Father Abraham, have mercy on me, and send Lazarus that he may dip the tip of his finger in water, and cool my tongue," was no prayer of the kind I have spoken of in the last chapter. The Rich Man was in earnest: he felt in need of what he asked for, and he desired to get it. Oh, how earnestly he desired! Never in his life-time had he so longed for anything. Perhaps as he lifted up his eyes, now no longer blinded by a veil of flesh, he saw the pure river of water of life, clear as crystal, proceeding out of the throne of God and of the Lamb,—that living water which Jesus gave to the woman of Samaria, and to so many others when He was on the earth—that water of which if a man drink he shall never thirst. I think he did. I think too, that he saw, though that river could never flow down to hell, yet that through the Lamb, out of whose throne it issued, it had flowed down to earth; nay more, had not only flowed down to earth, but had actually been flowing past him all the time that he was on earth. He had never heeded it; still for all that, day after day, month after month, year after year, he now knew that this pure river of water of life had been within his reach. He remembers too that many a time a voice had called him, saying, " Come ye to the waters." " Whosoever will, let him come and take of the waters of life freely." At the time he had paid no attention to the call: the water was flowing by him, but he had purple and fine linen, and sumptuous fare every day, and while surrounded by the rich viands of earthly luxury what need had he of living water? Never did he believe that the day could come when for a drop of that water he would have given a million times over all that he had ever had. But that day had come, and he believes it now: yea, he knows it; and oh how it increases his torment to remember that there was a time when he had only to stoop down and drink! Without money and without price he might have drunk abundantly of that water then, and if he had but drunk he never would have died. The Spirit of life was in the waters, and death temporal would have been the passage to life eternal. But the opportunity when he had it was lost, and he must now for ever endure his agony in " the pit where there is no water." (Zech. ix. 11.)

Oh, my brother, if you have not done it before, drink now of this water. In other words, I beseech you give yourself no rest until you have sought and found God. Again I tell you, you have not God by nature; and I will add, that you may have been baptized and a regular attendant for years at the Lord's table, and yet still be without God. Let there be no uncertainty about the matter with you; for he that has not God is unsaved.

With what earnestness and authority did the Apostle Paul preach this doctrine, and exhort the Corinthians to examine themselves, whether they had God. " Examine yourselves," he says, " whether ye be in the faith; prove your own selves. Know ye not your own selves how that Jesus Christ is in you, except ye be reprobates." (2 Cor. xiii. 5.) Now the meaning of this Scripture is solemn, very plain, and easily understood; there can be no mistake about it; it places all the world in two divisions, and so cuts the ground from under the feet of every other. In it the Holy Ghost tells us there are but two classes,—those in whom Christ is, and those who are reprobates. This is not the devil's teaching, and is most offensive to his people. The devil desires to make at least one other class: those who have no reason to think they have Christ, and yet think they have no reason to call themselves reprobates.

And into this third and most unscriptural class Satan has drawn multitudes. The great masses of professing Christendom are neither murderers, nor adulterers, nor drunkards, nor Sabbath breakers; they are not as a body outwardly profane or immoral: on the contrary, I believe that the greater portion of men are quietly labouring to get their own living, and are doing their duty tolerably as between man and man, in the position of life in which God has placed them. But yet multitudes of these men have not, and know they have not Christ; they would acknowledge it if you asked them, but in the same voice *they would deny that they were reprobates*: that is, only fit, like worthless dross (for that is

61

the meaning of the word), to be cast out of God's sight for ever. And yet God says, " Jesus Christ is in you, except ye be reprobates." Who then is the teacher that says a man can come short of having Christ, and not be reprobate? It is Satan, dear reader, it is Satan; and though a man may be as amiable, as moral, and as loveable as nature can make him; if he has not God, or, as the Apostle says, " If Christ is not in him," he is in the devil's division; and as reprobate silver is cast out by the refiner, so, if he dies as he is, will God cast him out. To my mind there is more likelihood of the conversion of publicans and prodigals, than of a class which, while it describes itself as not so good as it ought to be, places its hope of finding mercy on not being so bad as it might be,—a class, no member of which would dare to say he had got God; yet would dare to say he was not bad enough to be cast into hell.

He therefore who is not prepared to deny that the Bible is the Word of God, must acknowledge that the statement, " *Jesus Christ is in you, except ye be reprobates,*" closes every door of hope against the man who has not got God. " He that hath not the Son, hath not life," but " the wrath of God abideth on him."

Once more then I urge you, examine yourself as to whether you have God. Eternity is before you; sooner or later you know that you must enter on it, and you may be called to enter on it at any moment. If you can run the risk of such a call before you have a good Scriptural reason to believe that you have sought and found God, how great over you must be Satan's power. *Con-*

tentment without God was the sin of the Rich Man. He chose the world and the things of the world for his portion on earth, and you can do exactly what the Rich Man did if you please; but will it answer? Did it answer for him? For that sin he has been for upwards of eighteen hundred years lifting up his eyes in torments, vainly praying for water to cool his tongue. For that sin, amidst a multitude of other agonies, his irrevocable doom has become thirst,—thirst for that which God once offered him, yea, even besought him to accept, but for which he must now in the midst of unceasing torments pray, and for ever pray in vain.

Will you then, as God's Word has declared the Rich Man's portion to be prepared for every one who dies without Christ and reprobate, refuse to examine yourself as to whether you have got God?

But perhaps you know without examination that you have not. If this is so, it is by God's mercy that you are reading what you are, and you are exactly the sort of person into whose hands I wished my book to fall. You have not got God; you acknowledge that you have not, and *you are contented*! Contented with the good things, or in seeking after the good things of this life, although you are without God. Who gives you the power to be thus contented without God? Think! You know your contentment is not the peace of God: then whose contentment, whose peace must it be? Think, I say again: think. Is it not an awful power to possess —to be able to rest satisfied with the devil's contentment, and contented without God! Will you, can you, if you know you are without God, continue thus contented? What is it that you are getting in exchange for God? Whatever it is it is no doubt pleasant enough now, but what can it do for you in the hour of your soul's need? That hour looks far off perhaps, but it may come sooner than you expect. At all events it *is* coming. Esau sold his birthright for one morsel of meat, and you think he was a madman, yet are you not guilty of far greater madness if you sell your soul for the pleasures of sin, and take what the devil and the world can give you in exchange for God?

I feel much pressed in spirit while writing on this part of my subject. May God the Holy Ghost, for Jesus Christ's sake, bless it to all who read it. But I was myself once contented without God. My whole idea of happiness then consisted in spending my time agreeably. It was a pleasant day to me on which amusement after amusement prevented it from hanging heavily on my hands. But suddenly, during the days of this contentment, and in the midst of forgetfulness of God, I was taken ill, so ill that I thought I was going to die. I then learned something of what it was to be without God. Where was my contentment then? What could those things which up to that moment had been my joy and peace do for me then? What should I have cared for the whole world, if it had been offered to me then? I had no want then but one, and that want was *God*. O how willingly then would I have suffered the loss of all things, and, as the Apostle says, have counted them but "dung," if I could only have won Christ. My life itself would have been as nothing, if by laying down my life I could have got God. I was without God, and *felt it*, and everything was valueless except Him. For seven months I sought Him, but I could not find Him. Nature could not have stood much more, and my friends began to fear for my reason. But man's extremity is God's opportunity, and at last I had Scriptural warrant for believing that though He never would have been found of me if I had not first been found of Him, that for Christ's sake He had forgiven my sins, had given me His Spirit, and that I had got God. Still, do believe me when I tell you, that all I have ever known or imagined of agony never came up to the agony of the seven months in which I believed and felt myself to be without God. Conceive what are the sufferings of those who are without God, and feel it for ever and ever.

Now what happened to me may happen to you : you may be taken ill—and what happened to me may *not* happen to you—you may be taken ill, and *not* feel your want of God. Long before you die you may have rejected God once too often, and He may have sworn in His wrath that you shall never enter into His rest. In that case perhaps even your deathbed may be without terror. You may give directions about your funeral, take leave of your family with calmness, and then die quietly and in apparent peace. You may never feel your need of God until you are in hell; but should this be so, good would it have been for you if you had never been born. "Who among us shall dwell with the devouring fire? who among us shall dwell with everlasting burnings?" This is God's own question, by the mouth of the Prophet Isaiah; and the devouring fire and the everlasting burning must be the portion of all who die without God. To be without God is death; to be without God, and feel it, is a devouring fire, and will be an everlasting burning, unless it be quenched in the waters of life. This death man does not and cannot feel naturally, simply because he *is* dead: he must be spiritually quickened before he can feel spiritual things. But sooner or later every man will be spiritually quickened: this death sooner or later God has determined that every man shall feel. I believe that this is the death the Rich Man felt in hell, when he cried for water—I believe it is the death our precious Saviour felt, when forsaken of His Father He cried, "My God, My God, why hast Thou forsaken Me?" He was without God in the world, and felt it.—I believe this is the death every awakened sinner feels, when he cries for pardon and the Holy Spirit, before he believes in Jesus. *When he believes, his thirst is quenched; he gets God.* God is in him from that moment: "a well of water springing up into everlasting life."

Let no man say he does not know whether or not he has got God. Any man may answer this question for himself who will only take the trouble to read his Bible, with prayer for the teaching of the Holy Spirit. If he is not sufficiently anxious about the matter to read his Bible and pray for teaching, he may be perfectly sure that he has not got God.

The Bible says, " If any man is in Christ, he is a new creature: old things have passed away, all things have become new." If, on self-examination, you have reason to believe that your thoughts, desires, tastes, pursuits, and habits have undergone a transformation, so that your affections are now set on things above and not on things on the earth, you have Scriptural warrant for considering yourself a new creature. If not, what warrant have you for believing you have got God?

The Bible says, " They that are Christ's have crucified the flesh, with its affections and lusts." Now I do not tell you that in order to examine whether you have got God; you are to examine whether or not you have any sinful lusts and affections: " The lust of the flesh, the lust of the eye, and the pride of life," will remain, and make themselves felt in the best of men until their warfare is accomplished and death swallowed up in victory. But do you fight against these lusts? Examine yourself; for on this depends the evidence whether or not you have got God. If you are not crucifying the flesh, with its affections and lusts, what warrant have you for believing you have got God?

The Bible says " we " (that is Christians) " thus judge, that if one died for all, then were all dead: and that He died for all, that they which live should not live henceforth unto themselves, but unto Him which died for them, and rose again." (2 Cor. v. 14, 15.) Now, says St. Paul, this is the universal judgment of Christians,— that they should not live unto themselves, but unto Him who died for them; and it cannot require much self-examination to ascertain whether or not this is your judgment. Your life, your daily conduct is the answer both to yourself and others. You call yourself a Christian. If any doubted your Christianity, you would think he was uncharitable. But do you live unto yourself, or unto Him who you say died for you, and rose again? If you are living simply for self,—if your thoughts, words, and works have their primary reference, not to Christ's glory, but to your own well-doing in the world, what warrant have you for believing that you have got God?

To be brief, have you the Spirit of Christ? The Spirit of Christ led Him, when He was on the earth, to trust in the Lord, and go about doing good. Have you this Spirit, the Spirit of Christ? If you have not the Spirit of Christ you most certainly have not got God. On the other hand, if the things natural to the old man have so passed from you, that the affections and desires of your heart are more set on heavenly than on earthly things, —if you are crucifying the flesh and habitually living not unto yourself but unto Him who died for sinners,— you are doing what no man ever did, or ever could do by nature. Your frames, feelings, doubts, thoughts, fears, may be what they may, but you may be sure (and you dishonour the Lord Jesus Christ if you are not sure) that He who hath wrought for you this self same thing is God, who also hath given unto you the earnest of His Spirit. The tempers and dispositions of your mind are not what they were by nature. It is true that the flesh still lusteth against the Spirit, but it is a grief to you, for you have become *heavenly-minded*. Though with Paul you cry out, " Oh, wretched man that I am," with Paul also you can say, " I delight in the law of God after the inward man "; " with the mind I myself serve the law of God." Be of good cheer, dear brother: fight on, and fear not. The Spirit that is in you is God's Spirit, witnessing with your spirit that you have got God.

CHAPTER VI

God the only Hearer of Prayer

"FATHER ABRAHAM, send Lazarus, that he may dip the tip of his finger in water, and cool my tongue." Such was the earnest heart-felt prayer of the poor Rich Man; but its heart-felt earnestness could avail him nothing. His prayer was too late.

But there was another reason also, even if it had not been too late, why this prayer as put up by the Rich Man could never have been answered. Such a prayer would have availed him no more if offered up on earth, than it did when offered up in hell. It was not only too late, but it was addressed to a person who had no power to answer prayer. The man was in want, and his need was a need that in this world God not only promiseth, but delighteth to supply. The Scriptures abound with invitations to the poor and needy lacking water. To them "the Spirit and the Bride say, Come"; and to them, they who have accepted the invitation for themselves, are commanded to say, "Come"; to them are addressed the words, "Let him that is athirst come, and whosoever will, let him take of the water of life freely." But the same God, who without exception gives to every thirsty soul these most gracious invitations, tells them also to WHOM they must come for water. Not to saints, or angels, or the spirits of just men made perfect, but to the Lord Jesus Christ; to Him of whom, under the teaching of God's Spirit, the Samaritan woman asked water; to Him who in the temple stood and cried, " If any man thirst let him come unto ME and drink "; to Him who hath said, " Whosoever drinketh of the water that I shall give him, shall never thirst; but the water that I shall give him shall be in him a well of water, springing up into everlasting life." The Rich Man went to Abraham and asked him for water, and had he asked him for it when he was on the earth, Abraham would have been as unable to give it him, as he was when he asked him for it in hell.

This prayer addressed to Abraham is the only instance in Scripture of prayer being made to a saint; and though it bore no fruit in heaven, it has, like many other of the productions of hell, borne much on earth. Prayers to saints have become common now, and the Rich Man has had many disciples. But as God has declared HIMSELF the only Hearer and Answerer of prayer, and made a way, even through Jesus Christ His Son, by which sinners, even the chief, can go direct to Him, judge how such prayers must grieve and insult God.

When man sinned, and God in consequence left him, there was no way remaining open by which God and man could meet. Man's sin had separated, and apparently for ever, between God and man. No created intelligence either in heaven or hell could imagine any way by which it could be possible for these two, God and man, to be brought together in peace. There seemed a great gulf between them, to all finite wisdom as impassable on earth as is now the great gulf that is fixed between hell and heaven. Had things remained as they became when man sinned, there could have been no place found for repentance; for even assuming that man had felt sorry for his sin, and desirous of asking pardon, the sorrow and the desire could never have been made known to God, for man could not have got to God to tell Him of his penitence. The way to God, or, as it is typified in Scripture, "*the way into the holiest*," was barred by man's sin; and however much he might have desired it, there was no way by which man could get to God.

I believe it is in reference to this fact that the Holy Spirit uses the wonderful language of Isaiah lix. 16: "And the LORD saw it, and it displeased Him that there was no judgment; and He saw that there was no man, and wondered that there was no intercessor; therefore His arm brought salvation unto him, and His righteousness it sustained him." To God belonged mercies and forgiveness, though we had rebelled against Him, and He was not willing that any should perish. But how could a way be made by which man could present his prayer to God, and by which God could grant it when it was presented? God's own arm brought salvation unto man. Rather than leave us without an intercessor, or rather than that there should be no place where God and man could meet, God so loved the world that He gave His only begotten Son to take our nature upon Him. God was manifest in the flesh, and as man, endured the death which sin had entailed on man : not merely the death of the body, but the death of the soul,—for His soul was made an offering for sin : not merely the death of the body, but the being forsaken of God. As God left Adam for sin, so He left Christ. But the moment Christ was without God He felt it, and immediately, as I have said before, the cry burst from Him, " I thirst." I know we are told that Christ uttered this cry that " the Scriptures might be fulfilled "; but does anyone suppose that it had reference to the thirst of the body only. Ah, no! the great thirst of the Saviour was His thirst after God. To be without God is the penalty of sin; but when we are without Him, to feel it and to thirst for Him, is the work of the Holy Spirit. Never did the cry, "I thirst," go up from earth to God; or, in other words, never did man on earth feel his want of God, and cry for Him, without getting God. Christ went to the cross laden with sin,—sins, it is true, not His own, but His people's; still by these sins He who did no sin was made sin in God's sight. God saw sin on Christ, visited Him with its penalty, and forsook Him.

The agonizing cry that burst from the lips of Jesus, " My God, My God, why hast Thou forsaken Me?" reveals how in the very moment of His desertion " the sorrows of death compassed Him about, the pains of hell gat hold upon him." The Man Christ Jesus was without God. He who had heretofore been with Him always had left Him; and as the hart panteth for the water brooks, so thirsted His soul for the living God. He longed, as every man does who is without God and feels it, to follow after God until He found Him, and brought Him back to Him. And what did He do? Did He cry to Abraham to intercede for Him, or to Moses, who so often interceded when on earth for Israel? Did He ask Daniel, a man greatly beloved, to go to God and entreat Him to come back? No! If He had, Abraham, Moses, and Daniel would have known nothing of the prayer addressed to them, for the saints of God are neither omnipresent nor omniscient; and even had they, their holy spirits would have been grieved that a man should have addressed to them what He should only have addressed to God.

But the Man Christ Jesus in His hour of need prayed to neither advocate nor mediator. He was forsaken of God for the sin that God saw on Him, and in the moment that He was forsaken He felt it, and was athirst for God. But in the same moment of His need, from the head and hands and feet of Jesus began to flow BLOOD; it was that BLOOD, without the shedding of which there could have been no remission, but it was that BLOOD which the Scriptures declare cleanseth from ALL sin. When God saw that blood He saw no more sin on Christ, for that blood had made a full and sufficient sacrifice, satisfaction, and oblation: the sin on Him was all gone, washed all away in His own blood.

In the extremest hour of His need the Man Christ Jesus sought neither mediator nor advocate with God;

yet it is certain that He who was made sin for us, and for sin forsaken of God, sought and found a way to God, and prevailed to bring God back to Him. How did He do this? The Holy Spirit, by the mouth of Paul answers the question: "By His own blood." "BY HIS OWN BLOOD HE ENTERED IN ONCE INTO THE HOLY PLACE." (Heb. ix. 12.)

Glory be to God on high, on earth peace, good-will towards men. In Christ we see how God the Father devised a plan, which, by the Spirit of God, God the Son worked out, by which a man laden with sin could get rid of sin, find a way into the presence of that very God who had left him on account of sin, and prevail with Him to return to him.

When the blood of Christ was shed for sinners the veil of the temple was rent in twain; and now, says the Holy Ghost in another place (Heb. x. 19, 20), we have "boldness to enter into the holiest by THE BLOOD OF JESUS." When this "way" was opened, Christ's work was completed on earth, and when His work was completed, His people were complete in Him. He had finished the work that His Father had given Him to do, and as He cried, "*It is finished!*" He bowed His head, and gave up the ghost.

He was laid in the tomb; the third day He rose again, and at the appointed time ascended up where He was before. As the everlasting doors were lifted up, that the King of glory might come in, what were the first words addressed to Christ by God the Father? "*Sit Thou at My right hand.*" "Sit Thou at My right hand, until I make thine enemies Thy footstool "; but also, Sit Thou at My right hand as " the Man of my right hand,"—" the Man that is my Fellow,"—the Son of Man who is also the Son of God,—the Advocate with the Father,—the one Mediator between God and man. Oh, how the heart of Paul burned with holy faith and joy as he contemplated his acceptance with God, through the finished work and advocacy of this Mediator. " It is God that justifieth," he exclaims; " who is he that condemneth? It is Christ that died, yea, rather, that is risen again, who is even at the right hand of God, who also maketh intercession for us."

Christ is at the right hand of God. He has ascended up on high, leading captivity captive, and hath received gifts for men, " yea even for the rebellious also, that the Lord their God may dwell among them." (Psalm lxviii. 18.) He is at the right hand of God, " having received of the Father the promise of the Holy Ghost." (Acts ii. 33.) In virtue of His exaltation to the Mediatorial throne, God the Son has received from God the Father the gift of God the Spirit; and this gift " He has received for men, yea, even for the rebellious." He who is without God, and feels it on earth, can now go to the great God and our Saviour Jesus Christ, and get His need supplied; but the great God and our Saviour Jesus Christ brought back God to man, and made this way by which man could go to God, at the cost of His own blood. (Acts xx. 28.)

Think then, after the cross and passion, the death and burial, the glorious resurrection and ascension, and the exaltation to the Mediatorial throne purchased at such a price, how insulting it must be both to the Father and to the Son, and how grieving to God's Holy Spirit, when men seek other mediators and pray to other advocates and intercessors. " I am the Way, the Truth, and the Life," says Jesus. " No man cometh unto the Father but by ME."

Some will say, however, we do not go to *the Father* through other advocates and mediators, but *to the Son,* —asking such as James and Peter, or the beloved Disciple, or the blessed Virgin mother, to propitiate Him in our favour. First I would ask such, Do you think that anything or anybody could make Christ more willing to receive and save you than He is? Has He not purchased the power with His own blood? And then I would tell you that Christ and His Father are One, and that *the only way to the Father is the only way to the Son.* A man can no more approach Christ, except by the blood of Christ, than he can approach His Father.

" It was for the joy set before Him," says St. Paul, that Christ " endured the cross, and despised the shame "; and part of the joy set before Him was, that as the One Advocate between God and man, He might for ever sit down at the right hand of God, able to save to the uttermost all who come to God by Him. To deprive Him of this joy was the one great object of Satan, during all Christ's life on earth; and that he may hinder it yet, as far as he can, is his object still; hence his introduction of other ways to God, of other advocates, and other mediators. Again then I remind you

77

that the Rich Man's prayer is the only instance in Scripture of prayer being made to a saint. Never forget where it had its origin. Prayers to saints had their origin with the devil and his angels; were first offered by a lost soul in his agony, and came up direct from hell.

CHAPTER VII

Earnest, Heart-felt, Too-late Prayer

BUT not only was the prayer of the Rich Man addressed to the wrong person: it was also too late. Addressed to Abraham, or to any but God Himself, through Jesus Christ, it never could have availed anything. But there was a day when the way by which the Man Christ Jesus went Himself to God, was open to the Rich Man; and had he in that day, by the blood of Christ, gone in the name of Christ, and asked God for mercy, God would have listened to his prayer. Had he felt his need on earth as he felt it in hell, and cried to God on earth as he cried to Abraham in hell, God would have given him Christ, and Christ would have given him God.

Oh, what eager, longing, earnest, heartfelt prayers, are the prayers that are offered up in hell! With what strong crying and tears, and in what soul-agony are they uttered! How truly do the lips that pour them forth feel their need, and how anxious are they to get their prayers answered. Answered they can never be, however. The prayers and the sense of need are both alike unavailing; *they are too late.*

79

Terrible is the thought of praying a too-late prayer, and blessed for ever be our most merciful God, who has confined this terrible thing to hell. To this truth give all the Scriptures witness: that while in hell there is no place for hope, on earth there is no place for despair. On earth or in hell the need of the unsaved is the same, and that need God has typified in Scripture by a need of " water." There can be no hope in hell, because there is no water in hell (Zech. ix. 11); but to every thirsting soul on earth, thus saith the Lord: " When the poor and needy seek water, and there is none, and their tongue faileth for thirst, I, the Lord, will hear them; I, the God of Israel, will not forsake them. I will open rivers in high places, and fountains in the midst of the valleys: I will make the wilderness a pool of water, and the dry land springs of water." (Isa. xli. 17, 18.) When Jesus spake of living water, as He taught in the temple, St. John tells us that He meant the Holy Spirit; and God's promise in the Old Testament of water to the thirsty, is the same as Christ's promise under the Gospel dispensation,—that His Heavenly Father will give His Holy Spirit to all who ask Him. In the moment that a man asks on earth his need is all supplied, for God cannot deny Himself; and he who really asks receives; and he who receives the Holy Spirit receives Father, Son, and Holy Ghost,—his body becomes the temple of the living God,—he is born of the Spirit,—he has got God. All this is necessary for salvation, and all this can be done for a sinner on earth: but in hell there is no such thing as this.

Dear reader, whoever you are, if you have not yet repented, believed the Gospel, and received the Holy Ghost, I beseech you on the one hand not to despair, and on the other not to trifle with God. Now is your accepted time, NOW is your day of salvation. In the name of the Lord Jesus Christ, I NOW offer you water,—water that Christ called " living water,"—water, in receiving which you receive God, for the gift of this water is " the gift of God,"—water that shall be in you a well of water springing up unto eternal life, and of which, if you drink, you shall live for ever,—water flowing forth from THE ROCK that was smitten, and " that ROCK was Christ."

What say you? Will you accept this water now? Remember your need is the very same as the Rich Man's. If anybody could offer him water, what do you think could keep him from it? Then what keeps you? This: he feels his need, and you do not. Once he was like you. Once the warning to prepare to meet his God, and flee from the wrath to come, fell as idly on his ear as perhaps it does now on yours; but this was because he knew not God, and neither understood nor believed in His revealed Word. But now when he cries for water to cool his tongue, he understands and believes both in God and His Word; and oh, how closely would he follow any deliverer that could give him water. But there is no deliverer in hell. He cries, and cries, and cries, and yet there is none; and he must cry, and will continue to cry through the ages of eternity, and through the ages of eternity there will be no deliverer.

These thoughts are too frightful to dwell upon, yet are they truths clearly taught us in the Word of God, and now clearly felt and known to be truths by the wretched Rich Man. Reflect upon them, I beseech you, and pause before you refuse water NOW. Again I tell you your need is the very same as his, with this single difference: you are on earth, and he is in hell. He must remain in need for ever, *you can get yours supplied.*

Oh, you, whoever you are, if you are still unsaved, may God bless what I am writing to your salvation! Were it not that God's strength is made perfect in man's weakness, who could even attempt to save his fellow? for never does a Christian feel more impotent than when, either by speaking or writing, he is trying to make spiritual things touch and tell on unconverted men. But shall God's people, therefore, cease to try? God forbid. The command is—" Cast thy bread upon the waters." The promise,—" Thou shalt find it." If nothing less will do, I pray God that not only every unconverted man who reads this book, but every unsaved person on earth, may feel his want and need, as the Rich Man feels his in hell; I pray to God that the sorrows of death may even now compass him, that the pains of hell may immediately get hold upon him.

Does this wish scandalize you? Do you call it uncharitable, unscriptural, unchristian? If so, suspend your judgment, and let us consider together for a little the beginning of the 116th Psalm.

Earnest, Heart-felt, Too-late Prayer

PSALM CXVI

"I love the Lord, because He hath heard my voice and my supplications. Because he hath inclined His ear unto me, therefore will I call upon Him as long as I live.

"The sorrows of death compassed me, and the pains of hell gat hold upon me: I found trouble and sorrow. Then called I upon the name of the Lord; O Lord, I beseech Thee, deliver my soul."

Now in these verses we have a short but perfectly true history. They describe a case that really happened. They relate the experience of a man who is able to preface what he says by telling us that he loves the Lord: "I love the Lord," he says, and he tells us why: "I love the Lord, because He hath heard my voice and my supplications. Because He hath inclined His ear unto me, therefore will I call upon Him as long as I live." The writer of this had evidently been in some sore distress, and his distress had sent him with prayers and supplications to God. It is evident, too, that God had heard and answered his prayers, and that in consequence his heart so lately filled with anguish, was now filled with gratitude and love. But what was the heart agony that drove him to prayer? What was it that sent him with strong cryings and tears to God? It was, he himself tells us, the very same sorrows and pains that drove the Rich Man to cry for water: "The sorrows of death compassed me about, the pains of hell gat hold upon me: I found trouble and sorrow. THEN called I on the name of the Lord."

Now he who tells us all this was David, a man spoken of both in the Old and New Testament, as a man after God's own heart. The Lord dearly loved David; if He had not David would never have been able to say, " I love the Lord." " We love him," says St. John, " because He first loved us "; so that if any man loves the Lord he may be sure that the Lord loves him.

But how did the Lord show his love to David? By leaving him in the undisturbed enjoyment of purple and fine linen, and sumptuous fare every day? No. But by doing what I said just now I wished He would do to every unsaved man on earth,—by allowing the sorrows of death and the pains of hell to get hold of him: by sending him trouble and sorrow.

It was a sore dispensation that came upon David. We learn something of its terribleness from an expression in the eighty-eighth Psalm: "While I suffer Thy terrors I am distracted." But was this terrible distracted-ness really hurtful, or a proof of want of love on the part of God to David? No more, dear reader, than my wish is unscriptural and unchristian that you, if unsaved, may at once feel the want of the Rich Man. So far from want of love, this dealing of God with David was the greatest mercy that He could show him. It was the dealing of a wise Father with the child He loved; a dealing that in its consequences brought back that child to God. "THEN," says David, "THEN, when the sorrows of death compassed me about, and the pains of hell gat hold upon me, THEN called I upon the name of the Lord; O Lord, I beseech Thee, deliver my soul."

Terrible as they were in their experience, yet these sorrows of death and pains of hell were amongst the greatest blessings that ever God gave to David. Under a dispensation that the heart loveth—a time of ease and idleness—David had sinned against God; but now, when the dispensation is not joyous but grievous, David remembers again the God against whom he had sinned, and goes back to Him to save the soul his own wickedness had so well nigh destroyed.

"It was good for me," says David, "that I was afflicted."

Suppose David had never been afflicted. Suppose in this life his time of ease and idleness had never been interrupted. Suppose that, like the Rich Man, David had lived and died without a thought of death or hell, until the sorrows of a never dying death, and the pains of a never ending hell had compassed him about. I say suppose this. Had it been, do you think David would be thanking and blessing God for it now? By the mercy of God it was not so : but do you think David wishes that it had been? Do you think that now, as amidst the multitude who came out of great tribulation he stands and tunes his harp to praise, that David praises and glorifies with less loving adoration, because when he was on earth God visited him with the sorrows of death and pains of hell,—sorrows and pains that sent him to his knees with the prayer, "Oh, Lord, I beseech Thee, deliver my soul"? No, my dear brother, no; and neither will you by and by. You will one day acknowledge, whether you acknowledge it in heaven, earth, or hell, that it is better to suffer affliction with the people of God than to enjoy the pleasures of sin for a season. Even on earth God's people are the happiest: they have bread to eat that the world knows not of. Never did David feel such pleasure in his life as he felt when he could say, " I love the Lord."

The most pitiable object on earth is not the man whom the sorrows of death and pains of hell, or in other words the agonies of an awakened conscience, are leading to seek God,—but *an unsaved soul at peace*; and God's greatest curse out of hell is, to allow an unsaved soul to be at peace. If this curse is on you, I beseech you, ask God to remove it. Unless it is removed you cannot be saved, for unless it is removed you will remain *contented without God*. Consider which is best, to ask God now to send you the pain and trouble which shall send you to Him with David's petition, " Oh, Lord, I beseech Thee, deliver my soul "; or to wait for the pain and trouble which must sooner or later come upon you, and that will drive you to Abraham with the Rich Man's too-late prayer: " Send Lazarus, that he may dip the tip of his finger in water, and cool my tongue."

CHAPTER VIII

The Answer

BUT did the prayer of the Rich Man receive no answer? Yes: our Saviour has recorded that it did; and God has Himself said that all too-late prayers shall be answered. The prayer of the wretched Rich Man got the answer promised by God, and that answer was MOCKERY. Many are the passages in Scripture which tell us what Prov. i. 24 tells us,— " Because I have called, and ye refused; I have stretched out my hand, and no man regarded, but ye have set at nought all my counsel, and would none of my reproof; I also will laugh at your calamity, I will mock when your fear cometh." Abraham's answer to his prayer for water,—" Son, remember that thou in thy life time receivedst thy good things,"—was a fulfilment of this Scripture, and must have sounded in the ears of the Rich Man as the very essence of keenest mockery.

" Abraham said, SON." What bitter retrospection of privileges enjoyed, of opportunities neglected, must that first word have called up! And remember, that like all other Scripture, that word was written for our learning. "Abraham said, Son." What! A son of Abraham in hell! Can this be possible? And will Abraham himself, to whom the promises were made, acknowledge as his son one of the children of the wicked one? Yes: for no one knew better than did Abraham the distinction between an Israelite after the flesh, and the true descendants of that Seed in whom all the nations of the earth were to be blessed.

"It is the Spirit that quickeneth," saith the Lord Jesus; "the flesh profiteth nothing." The Rich Man was a son of Abraham after the flesh; he was born an Israelite, and doubtless on the day prescribed had been admitted into the Jewish Church by circumcision. It is likely he could say much as Paul said: "Circumcised the eighth day, of the stock of Israel, of the tribe of Benjamin, an Hebrew of the Hebrews." To him, as it was to the Pharisee when he went up to the temple to pray, it was a great comfort to think that he was not as other men: other men were sinners of the Gentiles, but he was an Israelite,— a son of the Church, a son of Abraham. What more did he require, for as a son of Abraham, a son of the Church, was he not a son of God? His conclusion was, as the conclusion of all such men is, that he was. It was a false conclusion, but he believed it. What many now believe of their baptism and Church privileges so he believed of his circumcision and Jewish privileges—that they made him a child of God; and to have taken from him his hope in these, would have been to have taken from him his whole religion. Well would it have been for him, however, if they had been taken from him, for as they were not, he lived and died under a strong delusion.

But how terribly was that delusion broken, when Abraham called him "SON" in hell. There, on every side of him, in that place prepared for the devil and his angels, he saw sons of Abraham, sons of the Church, but he saw not a son of God. There he learned that a son of the Church on earth might perish, for no other reason than that when on earth he had never been made a son of God. There he learned, that though on earth he had had great advantages, especially that unto him, as a child of Abraham, had been committed the Bible, "the Oracles of God," yet that these advantages were not in themselves salvation, but responsibilities; that through his own neglect he had turned that which should have been unto him a savour of life unto life into a savour of death unto death, and that so far from their having saved him, God would for ever hold him responsible for not having taken advantage of his advantages. There in hell he learned what he ought to have learned on earth, for it is the teaching of all Scripture, that he is not a son who is one outwardly, "neither is that circumcision which is outward in the flesh," and that neither descent from Abraham, nor any other spiritual advantage, can ever, without the spirit and faith of Abraham, make a son of the Church a son of God.

That a circumcised Jew, a descendant of Abraham, must of necessity be a child of God, was in ancient days the firmly believed faith of every Jew who was not a child of God; and the very same creed is held in our own day, by those who believe in the doctrine of baptismal regeneration: believe that every baptized person is, in virtue of his baptism, made what the English Church Catechism teaches him he is made: "a member of Christ, a child of God, and an inheritor of the kingdom of heaven." This doctrine, so boldly and unequivocally believed and taught now, was as boldly and unequivocally believed and taught in the days of our Saviour, and was by Him as boldly and unequivocally denied and refuted. "We are Abraham's seed," said the unregenerate Jews who went about to kill Jesus in the flesh, "and we have one Father, even God." "We are the children of the Church," say the unregenerate baptized, who go about to kill Jesus in the Spirit; "and we have one Father, even God." "I know that ye are Abraham's seed," said Jesus; I know that ye have been baptized into the Church: but ye are not the children of God. "Ye are of your father the devil." "If God were your Father, ye would love Me." Ye are Abraham's seed, ye are the children of the Church, but *if ye love not Me, ye are of your father the devil.* (John viii. 37, 42, 44.)

Dear reader, let no man deceive you; especially beware of that bad man and desperately wicked deceiver, your own heart. As God said to them of old time that there were two circumcisions,—the circumcision of the flesh and of the heart, and that true circumcision was "that of the heart, in the spirit, and not in the letter,"—so has He told us that there are two baptisms: the baptism of water, which is outward in the flesh, and the baptism of the Holy Ghost, which is inward in the spirit. The first, the baptism of water, we have almost all of us, I believe, received either in our infancy or since; but to say that every man who has been baptized with water must therefore of necessity have been baptized with the Holy Ghost, is not only false, but an absurdity. As well might every Israelite who was circumcised in the flesh have said that he must therefore of necessity have been circumcised in heart. Some did say so, and I have already shown how our Lord met and answered the doctrine. Let one more passage from God's Word, which amongst a multitude refutes not only in spirit but in the very letter such a belief, suffice to show that it is heresy. "The days come, saith the Lord, when I will punish all them which are circumcised with the uncircumcised; for all the nations are uncircumcised, and all the house of Israel are uncircumcised in the heart." (Jeremiah ix. 25, 26.)

The question then is, Have you been baptized with the Holy Ghost? Does God's Spirit witness with your spirit that you have? If so, then have you indeed been born again: then have you in very truth been made a member of Christ, a child of God, and an inheritor of the kingdom of heaven. Then, before the worlds were, God gave you to His Son, and neither man nor devil shall ever pluck you out of His Hands. Rejoice, and be exceeding glad; for now are you an Israelite indeed: the Eternal God is thy refuge, and underneath are the Everlasting Arms. You are a believer in the Lord Jesus Christ, and you HAVE everlasting life.

The Answer

But if you have not been baptized with the Holy Ghost, I tell you in all faithfulness that your baptism of water will profit you nothing. "Except a man be born of water and of THE SPIRIT, he cannot enter into the kingdom of heaven"; and if after having enjoyed for a lifetime the outward opportunities and Church privileges of a Christian, you die without having been baptized with the Holy Ghost, your opportunities and Church privileges will avail you no more than his sonship and circumcision availed the Rich Man. I will even go farther: your advantages being greater than his, entail on you a greater responsibility, so that you may expect them to sink you in an even lower hell.

But remember that when Abraham called the Rich Man "Son," he spoke to an unsaved son *in hell*. It shall be more tolerable for Sodom and Gomorrah *in the judgment* than for an unsaved son. But you have, however, not yet been called to judgment,— mercy and goodness still follow you; and an unsaved son on earth need not despair: God is yet willing to baptize YOU with His Spirit.

More than eighteen hundred years ago there was a man sent from God, whose name was John. He was sent to baptize with water and to point men to Christ. (John i. 6, 7, 31.) "Then went out to him Jerusalem, and all Judea, and all the region round about Jordan." Pharisees and Sadducees, Scribes, Publicans, soldiers, common people,—the circumcised and uncircumcised, the baptized and unbaptized,—all flocked round John the Baptist. And very anxious was he about the souls

of that multitude, and he baptized them because his
baptism was an ordinance of God; but did he preach to
them baptism? John the Baptist pointed the people,
not to the waters of baptism, but to the Lord Jesus
Christ. To one and all was his cry the same: " BEHOLD
THE LAMB OF GOD." And why, when John was specially sent to baptize with water, did he preach Christ,
rather than baptism? Because he knew that the one
great want of that vast multitude was a baptism with
which no man could baptize his fellow,—the baptism
of THE SPIRIT; and HE who sent him to baptize with
water, had revealed to John that it was CHRIST *who
baptized with the Holy Ghost."* (John i. 33.)

Reader, are you a minister? Your mission is the
same as was the mission of John the Baptist: to baptize
with water, and to point men to Christ.

Reader, are you a baptized unregenerate son of the
Church: born of water, but not of the Spirit? Again
I say you must not despair. Go to Jesus. " He shall
baptize you with the Holy Ghost." (Matt. iii. 11.)
May HE who taught John teach you.

I have dwelt long on the first word of Abraham's
answer to the Rich Man, and will say but little more on
the remainder. To me it sounds from first to last (and
I believe it sounded so to him) as bitter mockery; calcu-
lated, let him look at it as he might, to increase rather
than to allay his torment.

The first word was, " SON "; the next, " REMEMBER."
" Abraham said, *Son, remember.*" Oh, if it were not
for the hope of getting some poor sinner to " *remem-*

ber " before it is too late, I should shrink from putting on paper the thoughts that are rising in me. The lost in hell cry to heaven for water, and instead of water comes down the answer, " *Son, remember.*" It cannot be needful to tell them to remember; the wretched ones cannot help remembering, for remembrance is one of the torments, one of the never dying worms of hell; but still to have the prayer for water answered by being told to *remember*, oh, how it must add fuel to the flame !

Remembrance must be a frightful thing in hell ! We read in the Bible of many that were lost, unless indeed some of them were converted after Scripture is silent about them. What now must be their memories when they think of the things that they took in exchange for their souls ? What now must be the memories of Balaam and Achan, of Herod, Felix, and Agrippa, of Ananias and Sapphira, of Judas and Demas, or of the many others mentioned both in the Old and New Testament, who when on earth, like the young Ruler, turned their backs on God, because He called on them to sacrifice the world for the sake of heaven. Even were there no remembrance their misery would pass knowledge, for without a Mediator, without an Intercessor, they have fallen into the hands of the living God; and "it is a fearful thing to fall into the hands of the living God," for our God is a consuming fire. But God, judging from what He tells us in Scripture He will do, and from the answer He sent through Abraham to the Rich Man, does not scruple to add to the " consuming fire" "the sharp arrows of the Mighty, with coals of juniper." Abraham said, "Son"; then, "*Son, remember*"; and then, "SON, REMEMBER THAT THOU IN THY LIFE TIME HADST THY GOOD THINGS." The Rich Man asked for water, and he was told to remember; and not only to remember, but also specially what to remember. "Remember thy *good things*": the things that used to satisfy thee on earth, the things thou there madest thy gods, the things that have brought thee to thy place of torment. Thou knowest the value of Christ now, and that if thou couldst get Him, He could supply all thy need; but now thou canst never get Him: He is lost to thee for ever; still, son, thou hast this comfort: "*Thou in thy lifetime receivedst thy good things.*" Oh, now that he knew His value, to hear those things for which he had sold Christ called "*good things!*" Surely then was fulfilled in his ears the Scripture which saith, "He that sitteth in the heavens shall laugh: the Lord shall have them in derision." It is true that he himself once called the things for which he had lost Christ "*good*," and really thought them so good that he deliberately refused to give them up for Christ; but what did he think of them when he heard Abraham call them "*good*"? Do you think, if ever *you* are in the position of the Rich Man, that you will think the things "*good things*" that you now refuse to part with for Christ? Do you think any lost soul ever thought he had made a good bargain, or remembered such "*good things*" with anything but agony? Never forget while you are on earth that there will be *remem-*

brance in hell. Balaam remembers the day when he taught Balac to cast a stumbling-block before the children of Israel, and Balaam remembers too the day when Balac paid him for it. They were the wages of unrighteousness: but Balaam cared not for the unrighteousness, for he loved the wages, and called them "*good things.*" Balaam has since then been three thousand years in hell; with what feelings does he now remember the wages of unrighteousness? (Num. xxii,. xxiii., xxiv; Rev. ii. 14.)

Achan, the son of Carmi, remembers the day on which the walls of Jericho fell down. He remembers too that he helped to take the city, for he was fighting then on the Lord's side. He also remembers that he "saw amongst the spoils a goodly Babylonish garment, and two hundred shekels of silver, and a wedge of gold"; he recollects too that he "coveted them, and took them, and hid them in the midst of his tent." He knew that it was against the express command of God, but the temptation was so strong he could not resist it: the coveted things seemed to him then such "*good things.*" Achan, the son of Carmi, has since then been three thousand years in hell; with what feelings does he now remember the goodly Babylonish garment, the two hundred shekels of silver, and the wedge of gold? (Josh. vii.)

How now, as they receive the answer to their cry for water, "Remember that thou in thy lifetime receivedst thy good things," does Herod look on his brother Philip's wife, or his brother Philip's wife on

Herod; or how now do Felix and Agrippa remember the "*good things*" that kept them from salvation, when under the preaching of Paul, Felix trembled, and Agrippa was almost persuaded to become a Christian? What do you think is the value now that Judas puts on the thirty pieces of silver for which he betrayed Christ; or Demas on the world for which he forsook the service of God?

I leave you to answer these questions for yourself; only calling on you to recollect that the provision made in hell to satisfy the thirst of those who pray for water, is the remembrance of the "*good things*" for which on earth they sell Christ.

I shall say nothing about the portion of Lazarus: the "*evil things*" which he had on earth. It would have seemed in the eyes of all men, and most of all in his own, that "*evil things*" had come upon him, if the Rich Man when in this world had lost his purple and fine linen, if his property had passed away to another, and he himself, a beggar without health or friends, been laid side-by-side with Lazarus at what was once his own gate. But if those "*evil things*" had broken in upon his *contentment without God*, and so been made the means of setting him to seek God, would he not with a heart full of joy and gratitude be now blessing God for his earthly troubles; would he not smile now, as doubtless Lazarus does smile when he hears the name given them by Abraham: "*evil things*."

But there is one thing yet wanting to fill the Rich Man's cup, and Abraham supplies it before he ceases speaking. Had he said no more than that the Rich Man in his lifetime had had his good things, and likewise Lazarus evil things, but that now Lazarus was comforted while he was tormented, the bitterest of its bitter ingredients would have been spared him; for he might have looked forward to the day when he should have drunk it out to the very dregs. As his "*good things*" had come to an end, so also might he have hoped that some day or other would his "*evil things.*" It might not have been for years, perhaps not for many millions of years,—and many millions of years is a long time: but if Abraham had only left the Rich Man a hope that hell was not eternal,—that at some time, in the far, very far off distance, he might expect deliverance from his "*evil things*,"—hell would have ceased to be hell, for there would have been hope there; and the Rich Man might have comforted himself, as the people of God comfort themselves on earth, that every day his salvation was a day nearer: that any amount of *time* spent in affliction was still "a light affliction," compared to the joy before him in his ultimate and everlasting future.

But hell is eternal. If hell was not eternal our Saviour could not under any circumstances have said what He does say: that it would have been good for some men if they had never been born. Let hell be admitted to exist for as long a period as the mind of man can imagine, yet that imagined period would one day come to an end: and if at the end of that period hell was to be done away, and those who had been lost were to enter into the lot of the saved, great, surpassing knowledge, would have been to every man the gift of his being; for no matter through what sufferings he passed to it, he would have been born heir, and have been sure to succeed to *everlasting* glory.

But hell *is* eternal: and so Abraham told the Rich Man. Had he not added something to that on which I have already commented, the Rich Man might have had hope; but Abraham did add something, and that something left the cup of the lost all torment, without mixture, for it banished hope from hell. " And beside all this," said Abraham, " between us and you there is a great gulf fixed, so that they which would pass from us to you cannot, neither can they pass to us that would come from thence." Surely this was to clinch agony with agony, and to rivet it with despair. At the first he had been called to a retrospective remembrance; he is now called to a prospective. Before, he had been told to look back; Abraham now says, Look forward. You have looked back upon your " *good things*," now look forward upon your " *evil things*." Amongst other differences there is this one great difference between them : your " *good things* " were temporal, your " *evil things* " are eternal. " Between us and you there is a great gulf," and like Mount Zion, which cannot be removed, that gulf is FIXED. As surely as the dwelling place of the redeemed is everlasting, and as surely as the Lord is round about His people henceforth and for ever, so surely is the gulf that separates between you and heaven a FIXED GULF. Thus saith the Lord :

" Mount Zion cannot be removed, but abideth for ever "; and thus saith the same Lord : " Between us and you there is a great gulf fixed, so that they which would pass from us to you cannot, neither can they pass to us that would come from thence." (Psalm cxxv. 1, 2.)

Many write and speak now against the doctrine of eternal punishment; but all men, says St. Paul, " have not faith." Such men, not liking this, and much more of its teaching, try hard to explain away the plainest statements of the Bible. But the saved on earth and the lost in hell believe in the Word of God; and however much men and women of the world may hope and argue to the contrary, both God's people and devils know that *that Word is truth*; that holy men of old spake as they were moved by the Holy Ghost; and that what God has revealed by the mouth of His Apostles and Prophets is as unchangeable as God Himself. The gulf between heaven and hell is fixed; and everlasting punishment is as certain as everlasting glory. Both rest on the truth of God, and he who undermines the foundation of the one, undermines the foundation of the other. The devils believe hell to be everlasting, because they believe God's Word, and the devils believe and tremble. If you are unsaved you would tremble too if you believed God's Word; the only reason why you do not tremble is because you are an unbeliever.

You will be a believer some day. If you never believe on earth, you will believe in hell.

CHAPTER IX

The Second Petition

" BETWEEN us and you there is a great gulf fixed, so that they which would pass from hence to you cannot, neither can they pass to us that would come from thence." With the declaration of this most awful truth Abraham ceases to speak, and the Rich Man prays again.

Then he said, "I pray thee therefore, father, that thou wouldest send him to my father's house, for I have five brethren, that he may testify unto them, lest they also come into this place of torment."

Now there can be no doubt that the Rich Man was genuinely anxious that what he prayed for should be done; for, common as it is on earth, people in hell never commit the sin of praying for what they do not want. Why then was it that he had suddenly become anxious about his brethren? When he was with them in his father's house he never thought about their souls; why does he think about them now? Why, when he had never prayed for them on earth, does he pray for them in hell; beseeching that Lazarus might be sent to testify to them, lest they also should come into that place of torment?

My own belief is that there can be but one answer to the question. It is clear that it was not love, for there can be no love in hell; especially can there be no love to the souls of men; but the Rich Man had learned in hell, what had never probably occurred to him on earth,—that when he succeeded to his father's properties—to his purple and fine linen and sumptuous fare— he also succeeded to his father's responsibilities; and that amongst the many things with which God had then intrusted him, had been the souls of his tenants, his dependents, his household, and especially of his younger brethren. Like the unjust steward, however, he had been unfaithful to his trust, and instead of endeavouring to train for heaven those over whom he had been made head, he had set before them as a pattern the most corrupting thing on earth,—*the example of a man who was contented without God.* The poisoning powers of this example had no doubt more or less tainted his whole neighbourhood, and specially his own household, and the younger members of his family. Under its influence his five brothers had grown up into his likeness, and while he was praying for them in hell, they were living as he had lived on earth, and would, unless they were changed before they died, go where he went when he died. Well did their elder brother know this: but this was not why he prayed for them; he knew, besides this, what concerned himself more personally,—he knew, that though if they perished his younger brothers would be without excuse, yet that in a certain sense he had been on earth their keeper; that, Cain like, in consequence of the way he had discharged his keepership, his brothers' blood was on his head, and that so sure as he and his five brothers were shut up together for eternity, he would through eternity be shut up with five more torturers and tormentors. Hence his prayer.

When once a lost soul has lifted up its eyes being in torments, and realized the eternity of hell, it could hardly be conceived that its cup of suffering was not full, or that the intensity of its agony could know farther increase. But I believe this to be but earthly judgment,—the judgment of those who cannot see afar off. I believe that the Rich Man who had cried for water, and who had learned from Abraham that not only could he get no water, but that his torments were to be everlasting, knew also that there was yet *one thing* that could make even his torments more terrible; and I believe that his prayer, while it bore the appearance of anxiety for his brethren, was in reality a petition for himself,— a prayer for deliverance from that *one thing. The one thing that can add agony to the agony of the lost is, the being shut up for ever in hell with those they have helped to bring there.* It was the dread of this torment that was in the heart of the Rich Man; it was the dread of this torment that called forth his prayer. Well did he know that their reproaches, their revilings, and the persecutions of their undying vindictiveness, would be added to his other agonies, if once his five brothers came into that place of torment.

Oh, ye that are neglecting souls intrusted to your

care by God, lay to heart what I am saying. Think not only of the curse you are bringing on others,—on those to whom you ought to be a blessing,—but the curse you are bringing on yourself.

Oh, ye fathers! ye who train your sons, if not nominally yet virtually, to seek the things of the world before the things of God, in the name of the Lord Jesus Christ I say unto you, *Beware!* If you die with this sin on you, you will have your portion amongst the lost; and then in your agony how earnestly will you pray the prayer of the Rich Man: "Send Lazarus to my sons." Through following your training they may have gained the whole world; but full well will you know in hell, that if they enter there, their having gained the whole world will not help you to face your sons.

Oh, ye mothers! ye who train your daughters, if not nominally yet virtually, to seek the things of the world before the things of God, in the name of the Lord Jesus Christ I say unto you, *Beware!* If you die with this sin on you, you will have your portion amongst the lost; and then in your agony how earnestly will you pray the prayer of the Rich Man: "Send Lazarus to my daughters." Through following your training they may have gained the whole world, but full well will you know in hell, that if they enter there, their having gained the whole world will not help you to face your daughters.

Oh, ye masters of servants and schools; ye owners of mills and factories; ye proprietors of mercantile and other large establishments; ye employers, whoever ye are, of the heads and hands of your fellow creatures,—in the name of the Lord Jesue Christ I say unto you, *Beware!* God demands that you should take an interest in the souls of those that serve you. Live and die taking no interest in their souls, and you will take an interest in them in hell, where all who take no interest in souls on earth are certain, sooner or later, to be praying the prayer of the Rich Man.

But, above all, oh, ye careless, godless, ministers! ye hireling shepherds! ye who have solemnly taken God to witness that you believed yourselves called by the Holy Ghost to take on you the office of a Minister of Christ, while you knew all the while that you were taking it on you to serve your own earthly purposes; ye who have not lied unto men only, but unto God,—in the name of the Lord Jesus Christ I say unto you, *Beware!* If you die with your sins upon you, God alone knows into what depths they will sink you; but out of those depths, even though they be in the lowest hell, will you pray: " Send some one to testify to my congregation, lest they also come into this place of torment." It will be too late then: but for all that, in your despair you *will* pray. But, oh, what a word have I even for you, the chief of sinners: IT IS NOT TOO LATE NOW. It is not too late either for you or your congregation. Pray for yourself and your congregation *now*; in the name of the Lord Jesus Christ lay both yourself and them before God *now*; honestly seek, by pure Gospel word and work, to save both yourself and them *now*; and let your past have been what it may, you have the Word of God (1 Tim. iv. 16) that "in doing this thou shalt both save thyself and those that hear thee." But again I say unto you, *Beware!* Especially, situated as you are, *beware of delay*! Delay a little longer; delay until men are saying of you, what they once said of the Rich Man, "*He is dead*," and your prayer then will be too late; you will then be in hell, not only with your own blood, but with the blood of your people on your head. In the name of the Lord Jesus Christ, then, once more I say, *Beware!* and may the Lord Jesus Christ forgive you, have mercy on you, and turn you. Woe to you if He does not; for I do not believe there exists a more miserable being, even amongst the lost themselves, than a lost minister shut up in hell with his congregation.

And now let us consider the answer of Abraham to this second petition. The Rich Man had prayed, " Send Lazarus to my father's house, for I have five brethren, that he may testify unto them, lest they also come into this place of torment." " Abraham saith unto him, They have Moses and the Prophets, let them hear them."

Now it is quite evident, both from the prayer and its answer, that not only in the judgment of their elder brother, but in the judgment also of Abraham, these five brethren were unsaved; that while the brother was praying for them in hell, they were living in sin on the earth. What particular form of sin we know not, neither is it needful that we should know; suffice it, that as their brother had done before them, they were walking after the imaginations of their own hearts; were contented without God in the world, and would if they died perish as he did.

Yet how different was the answer now received by the Rich Man, to the answer given by Abraham to his first prayer. The answer to the first prayer shut at once and for ever the door of hope against himself; the answer to his second, though it refused his particular request, declared a sure and certain way by which his five godless brethren might be saved. "*They have Moses and the Prophets, let them hear them.*" I suppose I need not stop to tell you that when Abraham said, "They have Moses and the Prophets," he meant that they had the Scriptures, THEIR BIBLES.

Now whoever you are into whose hands this book has fallen, I trust you are quite clear about this one Scriptural truth,—that there is no other possible way by which *any man* can be saved except by FAITH: that is, by rejecting his own reasonings, wisdom, and carnal senses, and by *hearing* (to use the word used by Abraham), that is, by receiving, believing, and attending in their stead to what the Scriptures tell him. These Scriptures teach that men are justified " by the hearing of faith "; and again, that " faith cometh by hearing, and hearing by the Word of God." In other words, faith is hearing the Word of God, and believing it. The Rich Man prays, Send Lazarus that he may testify to my brothers. Abraham answers, Your brothers have got the Scriptures: let them attend to what they testify.

And what do the Scriptures testify? Let Scripture

answer for itself. " THE TESTIMONY OF JESUS IS THE SPIRIT OF PROPHECY." The whole spirit of the Scriptures is the testimony of Jesus. For this one purpose, and for this one purpose only, were they written,— that they might testify of Jesus Christ the Son of God; and had not God so loved the world as to give us Jesus, not only there never would, but there never could have been a Bible. From Genesis to Malachi, and again from Matthew to Revelation, the Bible is one continuous testimony of God 'manifest in the flesh: a Saviour promised, and a Saviour given. No matter who is the author of the particular book or portion, the one theme of all Scripture is JESUS. Sometimes He may be spoken of typically, sometimes spiritually, sometimes literally, but still it is JESUS. Jesus ordained to come, Jesus coming, Jesus come; Jesus living, Jesus tempted, Jesus suffering; Jesus fulfilling all righteousness, Jesus forsaken of God and man; Jesus dying, Jesus buried, Jesus rising, Jesus ascending, Jesus exalted at the right hand of God; Jesus a Prince, Jesus a Saviour; Jesus receiving from the Father the Holy Ghost, and shedding Him forth on men, that the Lord their God might dwell among them; Jesus able to save, Jesus willing to save: to save not only the Rich Man's brothers, but all who come unto God by Him; Jesus the Alpha, Jesus the Omega; Jesus the Beginning, Jesus the Ending; Jesus the Author, Jesus the Finisher; Jesus the First, Jesus the Last. No matter whether written by Moses, the Prophets, or the Apostles of our Lord and Saviour, the one subject of the Bible is the Man Christ Jesus, " who is over all, God blessed for ever." (Rom. ix. 5.) The testimony of Jesus is the spirit of prophecy, therefore thus saith the Lord Himself, " Search the Scriptures," for Moses wrote of Me, David wrote of Me, the Prophets wrote of Me, and they are they which testify of ME.

Hell deserving sinners were these five brethren of the Rich Man, but they had Moses and the Prophets, and in Moses and the Prophets they had that which taught them not only how they might get their sins forgiven, but how they might attain when forgiven to *an immediate and perfect righteousness.* Oh, wonderful Word of God, declared by the mouths of holy men of old ! By faith in Christ Jesus the chiefest sinner may not only obtain a gift of pardon, but also " a gift of righteousness ": a gift of a righteousness so sinless and so pure, that the Word which declares it calls it, " THE RIGHTEOUSNESS OF GOD."

Think not these are my own comments on Moses and the Prophets; they are the words of God, by the mouth of the Apostles of our Lord and Saviour. Let Peter's commentary satisfy as to the truth of my first statement; let Paul's be sufficient for my second. " To HIM," says Peter, " give ALL THE PROPHETS WITNESS, that through faith in His name whosoever believeth in Him shall receive remission of sins "; and, " Now the righteousness of God without the law," says Paul, " is manifested, BEING WITNESSED BY THE LAW AND THE PROPHETS : even the righteousness of God, which is by faith of Jesus Christ, unto all and upon all them that believe; for there is no difference, for all have sinned and come short of the glory of God." (Acts x. 43; and Rom. iii. 21, 22, 23.) As sure then as Peter and Paul are correct in their interpretation of the Old Testament, so sure is it that in Moses and the Prophets was offered to these five brethren " *remission of sins,*" and " *the righteousness of God, which is by faith of Jesus Christ.*" And more than that, what was offered to these five brethren is offered to all who have a Bible.

God, knowing that the day was coming when the whole earth must stand before Him in judgment, " looked down from heaven upon the children of men, to see if there were any that did understand and seek God "; and His own testimony after the scrutiny was, " They are all gone aside, they are altogether become filthy; there is none that doeth good, no not one." (Psalm xiv. 2, 3.) Now God is not willing that any should perish, and in the moment that He saw that no flesh could be saved, but *because all had sinned and come short,* He must, as a just Judge, condemn them all in the judgment day, His wisdom was taxed to devise a way by which guilty man might stand before Him guiltless, and He be enabled, as a strictly just God, not only to let him pass without condemnation, but to recognize his title to an inheritance in the kingdom of heaven. And His wisdom *did* see a way, and His love made a way, and His Scriptures declare that way, and that way is JESUS.

God so loved the world, that when the fulness of the time was come, He sent forth His Son, made of a woman, made under the law, to redeem them that were under the law; and this is a faithful saying, and worthy of all acceptation, that Christ Jesus came into the world to save sinners. He who in the beginning was with God, and who was God, was made flesh, that He by the grace of God might taste death for every man. He was wounded for man's transgressions, He was bruised for man's iniquities, His blood was poured out to make an Atonement for man's soul; and the soul of Him who knew no sin was made an offering for man's sin. He who being in the form of God thought it not robbery to be equal with God, made Himself of no reputation, and took upon Him the form of a servant, and was made in the likeness of man; and being found in fashion as a man, He humbled Himself, and became obedient unto death, even the death of the cross. Thus it is written in Moses and the Prophets; and thus it behoved Christ to suffer, and to rise from the dead the third day; and that repentance and remission of sins should be preached in His name among all nations. (John iii. 16; Gal. iv. 4; 1 Tim. i. 15; John i. 1 and i. 14; Heb. ii. 9; Isaiah liii. 5; Lev. xvii. 11, and Matt. xxvi. 28; Isaiah liii. 10; Philip. ii. 6, 8; Luke xxiv. 46.)

JESUS CHRIST, A PERSON,—God manifest in the flesh, —living and dying for sinners : living for them that His life of sinless obedience might be imputed to them, as if they themselves had lived it; or, to quote one of the many ways in which St. Paul expresses the same thing, " that by the obedience of ONE many might be made righteous "; and dying for them, to make an Atonement for their sins, that His death and Atonement might be imputed to them, as if they themselves had died that death, and made that atonement, is the great DOCTRINE of Moses and the Prophets. Interpreted to us by Christ Himself and His Apostles, the Scriptures of the Prophets declare that the believer in Jesus, though in himself utterly without righteousness, and only worthy of everlasting death, shall not only, for the sake of Christ's death imputed to him, never be punished with death, but for the sake of Christ's righteousness imputed to him, shall be made " the righteousness of God in Him." While the great *subject* of Moses and the Prophets is JESUS, the great *doctrine* of Moses and the Prophets is SUBSTITUTION.

Abraham said to the Rich Man, " They have Moses and the Prophets." And what said the Rich Man? Did he thank God, and take courage, at least having hope that through reading and believing the Scriptures his brethren might not come to that place of torment? No! for from the day that the Old Serpent deceived Eve until this hour, both on earth and in hell has it always been the habit of the devil and his children to deny the all-sufficiency of the pure and unaided Word of God to save souls. " Abraham said, They have Moses and the Prophets." The Rich Man said, " Nay, father Abraham, but if one went unto them from the dead they would repent."

In this answer of the Rich Man we have the embodiment of that great lie which in different forms and shapes is now so openly held and taught not only by

the Church of Rome, but by multitudes of the clergy
and laity of the Church of England, and I fear even by
some ministers and others, from whose professed Evangelical creeds we might expect better things. It denies,
as they do, that if a man has got a Bible, he has got the
only teacher he requires. It denies, as they do, the
sufficiency of Scripture, when left without note, com-
ment, interpreter, or helper in the hands of a man, to
make him wise unto salvation. Abraham evidently im-
plied, not only that the five brethren might yet be
saved, but that, having Moses and the Prophets, they
had all that was necessary to teach them what they
must do to be saved. But what Abraham so directly
taught, the Rich Man as directly contradicted. " *Nay,
father Abraham.*" Nay, not so: I know they have
Moses and the Prophets; I know they have their Bibles,
the written Word of God; but by itself the Bible is not
sufficient: they must have some other teacher; the
Word of God, if left in their hands alone, will never
keep them out of this place of torment: if a little more
than God has already done was done to save them,—if
they had some great teacher, or helper of authority,—
if especially one went unto them from the dead, they
would repent.

Reader, if ever this thought rises up in your heart,—
that the Bible, if you read it with prayer for the teaching of God's Holy Spirit, is not able in itself to make
you wise unto salvation, remember, as I told you to
remember about the prayers addressed to saints and
mediators, where this lie first originated. It originated

in hell; and though God forbid that I should tell any man to refuse the help of his Church, his pastor, or of any teacher he thinks likely to help him, I DO tell him that he is to carry the doctrines of his Church and his other instructors to his Bible, and prayerfully compare their teaching with its teaching, before he receives it. "Though we or an angel from heaven," says St. Paul to the Galatians, "preach any other Gospel unto you than that we have preached unto you, let him be accursed"; thus plainly implying that a man is bound not only to test the teaching of his minister by his Bible, but, even if one appeared to him, the teaching of an angel from heaven; and also that if through un-questioning reliance on any teacher a man believes false doctrine, he would be without excuse, and—along with his false teacher,—"*be accursed.*" Had it pleased God to send Lazarus to these five brethren, they would have been bound to test all he said by Moses and the Prophets.

It is a solemn truth that Paul tells the Corinthians, and one of the first that the natural man has to receive: namely, that "the preaching of the cross is *to them that perish* foolishness." (1 Cor. i. 18.) Observe, it is not that they pretend to think it foolishness, but that they really do; and the last counsel that an unconverted man would give a friend in need would be to study his Bible. I believe the Rich Man most sincerely thought that if Lazarus went to them from the dead it would be far more likely to bring his brothers to repentance, than to read Moses and the Prophets; but his sincerely thinking so did not make it true. The Rich Man was under the devil's teaching, as every man is who is not taught of God, and consequently under "a strong delusion to believe a lie"; and there exists not on this earth a thing more offensive to God, or destructive to himself, than the honest, genuine belief of the natural heart of man. Men have been known to gain the whole world by their wisdom and natural powers, but no man ever yet followed the guidance of his own wisdom, from his birth to his grave, who did not dishonour God and lose his own soul. It was for this reason,—because no man could by wisdom find out God,—that God gave us His Word, the Bible; and whether we believe that Word or our own reason, is the point on which hangs our salvation.

As is always the case, he who was taught of God was right, and he who judged after the reasonings of his own heart wrong. "They have Moses and the Prophets," said Abraham. To send Lazarus to your brethren, even were there no other reason against it, would do no good, for "if they hear not Moses and the Prophets, neither would they be persuaded though one rose from the dead."

Six Short Rules for Young Christians

by BROWNLOW NORTH

I. Never neglect daily private prayer; and when you pray, remember that God is present, and that He hears your prayers. (Heb. xi. 6).

II. Never neglect daily private Bible-reading and when you read, remember that God is speaking to you, and that you are to believe and act upon what He says. I believe all backsliding begins with the neglect of these two rules. (John v. 39).

III. Never let a day pass without trying to do something for Jesus. Every night reflect on what Jesus has done for you, and then ask yourself. What am I doing for Him? (Matt. v. 13-16).

IV. If you are in doubt as to a thing being right or wrong, go to your room, and kneel down and ask God's blessing upon it. (Col. iii. 17). If you cannot do this, it is wrong. (Rom. xiv. 23).

V. Never take your Christianity from Christians, or argue that because such and such people do so and so, that therefore you may. (2 Cor. x. 12). You are to ask yourself, How would Christ act in my place? and strive to follow Him. (John x. 27).

VI. Never believe what you feel, if it contradicts God's Word. Ask yourself, Can what I feel be true, if God's Word is true? and if *both* cannot be true, believe God, and make your own heart the liar. (Rom. iii. 4; 1 John v. 10, 11).

Are You Asleep?*

J. C. Ryle

"Awake thou that sleepest."—EPHES. V. 14.

I PUT before you now a simple question. Look through the pages of this paper and you will soon see why I ask it. *"Are you asleep about your soul?"*

There are many who have the name of Christians, but not the character which should go with the name. God is not King of their hearts. They mind earthly things.

Such persons are often quick and clever about the affairs of this life. They are, many of them, good men of business, good at their daily work, good masters, good servants, good neighbours, good subjects of the Queen: all this I fully allow. But it is the eternal part of them that I speak of; it is their never dying souls. And about that, if a man may judge by the little they do for it, they are careless, thoughtless, reckless, and unconcerned. *They are asleep.*

I do not say that God and salvation are subjects that never come across their minds: but this I say,—they

---

* This address by a friend of Brownlow North's has been added to this edition of *The Rich Man and Lazarus* in order to make the book an economical and convenient size.

have not the uppermost place there. Neither do I say that they are all alike in their lives; some of them doubtless go further in sin than others: but this I say,—they have all turned every one to his own way, and that way is not God's. I know no rule by which to judge of a man's estate but the Bible. Now when I look at the Bible I can come to only one conclusion about these people: *they are asleep about their souls.*

These people *do not see the sinfulness of sin, and their own lost condition by nature.* They appear to make light of breaking God's commandments, and to care little whether they live according to His law or not. Yet God says that sin is the trangression of the law,—that His commandment is exceeding broad,—that every imagination of the natural heart is evil,—that sin is the thing He cannot bear, He hates it,—that the wages of sin is death, and the soul that sinneth shall die. Surely *they are asleep.*

Is this the state of your soul? Remember my question. ARE YOU ASLEEP?

These people *do not see their need of a Saviour.* They appear to think it an easy matter to get to heaven, and that God will of course be merciful to them at last, some way or other, though they do not exactly know how. Yet God says that He is just and holy, and never changes,—that Christ is the only way, and none can come unto the Father but by Him,—that without His blood there can be no forgiveness of sin,—that a man without Christ is a man without hope,—that those who would be saved must believe on Jesus and come to Him, and that he who believeth not shall be damned. Surely *they are asleep!*

Once more I say, is this the state of your soul? Remember my question. ARE YOU ASLEEP?

These people *do not see the necessity of holiness.* They appear to think it quite enough to go on as others do, and live like their neighbours. And as for praying and Bible-reading, making conscience of words and actions, studying truthfulness and gentleness, humility and charity, and keeping separate from the world, they are things they do not seem to value at all. Yet God says that without holiness no man shall see the Lord,—that there shall enter into heaven nothing that defileth, —that His people must be a peculiar people, zealous of good works. Surely *they are asleep!*

Once more I say, is this the state of your soul? Remember my question. ARE YOU ASLEEP?

Worst of all, these people *do not appear to feel their danger.* They walk on with their eyes shut, and seem not to know that the end of their path is hell. Some dreamers fancy that they are rich when they are poor, or full when they are hungry, or well when they are sick, and awake to find it all a mistake. And this is the way that many dream about their souls. They flatter themselves they will have peace, and there will be no peace; they fancy that they are all right, and in truth they will find that they are all wrong. Surely *they are asleep!*

Once more I say, is this the state of your soul? Remember my question. ARE YOU ASLEEP?

If conscience pricks you, and tells you you are yet asleep, what can I say to arouse you? Your soul is in awful peril. Without a mighty change it will be lost. When shall that change once be?

You are dying, and not ready to depart,—you are going to be judged, and not prepared to meet God,— your sins are not forgiven,—your person is not justified, —your heart is not renewed. Heaven itself would be no happiness to you if you got there, for the Lord of heaven is not your friend: what pleases Him does not please you; what He dislikes gives you no pain. His word is not your counsellor; His day is not your delight; His law is not your guide. You care little for hearing of Him: you know nothing of speaking with Him. To be for ever in His company would be a thing you could not endure; and the society of saints and angels would be a weariness, and not a joy. At the rate you live at, the Bible might never have been written, and Christ might never have died, the Apostles were foolish, the New Testament Christians madmen, and the salvation of the Gospel a needless thing. Oh, awake! and sleep no more.

Think not to say *you cannot believe your case is so bad, or the danger so great, or God so particular.* I answer,—the devil has been putting this lying delusion into people's hearts for nearly six thousand years. It has been his grand snare ever since the day he said to Eve, "Ye shall not surely die." Do not be so weak as to be taken in by it. God never failed yet to punish sin, and He never will: He never failed to make His word good, and you will find this to your cost, one day, except you repent. Reader, awake: awake!

Think not to say *you are a member of Christ's Church, and therefore feel no doubt you are as good a Christian as others.* I answer,—this will only make your case worse, if you have nothing else to plead. You may be written down and registered among God's people: you may be reckoned in the number of saints; you may sit for years under the sound of the Gospel; you may use holy forms and even come to the Lord's table at regular seasons; and still, with all this, unless sin be hateful, and Christ precious, and your heart a temple of the Holy Ghost, you will prove in the end no better than a lost soul. A holy calling will never save an unholy man. Reader, awake: awake!

Think not to say *you have been baptized, and so feel confident you are born of God, and have His grace within you.* I answer,—you have none of the marks which St. John has told me, in his first epistle, distinguish such a person. I do not see you confessing that Jesus is the Christ,—overcoming the world,—not committing sin,— loving your brother,—doing righteousness,—keeping yourself from the wicked one. How then can I believe that you are born of God? If God were your Father, you would love Christ: if you were God's son, you would be led by His Spirit. I want stronger evidences. Show me some repentance and faith; show me a life hid with Christ in God; show me a spiritual and sanctified conversation: these are the fruits I want to see, if I am to believe you have the root of the matter in you, and are a living branch of the true vine. But without these your baptism will only add to your condemnation. Reader, awake: awake!

I speak strongly, because I feel deeply. Time is too short, life is too uncertain, to allow of standing on ceremony. At the risk of offending, I use great plainness of speech. I cannot bear the thought of hearing you condemned in the great day of assize; of seeing your face in the crowd on God's left hand, among those who are helpless, hopeless, and beyond the reach of mercy. I cannot bear such thoughts,—they grieve me to the heart. Before the day of grace is past, and the day of vengeance begins, I call upon you to open your eyes and repent. Oh, consider your ways and be wise. Awake: awake! Why will ye die?

This day, as the ambassador of Christ, I pray you to be reconciled to God. The Lord Jesus who came into the world to save sinners,—Jesus the appointed Mediator between God and man,—Jesus who loved us and gave Himself for us,—Jesus sends you a message of peace: He says, " Come unto Me."

" Come " is a precious word indeed, and ought to draw you. You have sinned against heaven: heaven has not sinned against you. Yet see how the first step towards peace is on heaven's side. It is the Lord's message: " Come unto Me."

" Come " is a word of *merciful invitation*. Does not the Lord Jesus seem to say, "Sinner, I am waiting for you : I am not willing that any should perish, but that all should come to repentance. As I live, I have no pleasure in the death of him that dieth. I would have all men saved and come to the knowledge of the truth. Judgment is my strange work,—I delight in mercy. I offer the water of life to every one who will take it. I stand at the door of your heart and knock. For long time I have spread out my hands to you. I wait to be gracious. There is yet room in my Father's house. My long-suffering waits for more of the children of men to come to the mercy-seat before the last trumpet is blown, —for more wanderers to return before the door is closed for ever. Oh, sinner, come to Me!"

" Come " is a word of *promise and encouragement.* Does not the Lord Jesus seem to say, " Sinner, I have gifts ready for you: I have something of everlasting importance to bestow upon your soul. I have received gifts for men, even for the rebellious. I have a free pardon for the most ungodly,—a full fountain for the most unclean,—a white garment for the most defiled,— a new heart for the most hardened,—healing for the broken-hearted,—rest for the heavy-laden, joy for those that mourn. Oh, sinner, it is not for nothing that I invite you! All things are ready. Come: come unto Me."

Hear the voice of the Son of God. See that you refuse not Him that speaketh. Come away from sin, which can never give you real pleasure, and will be bitter at the last; come out from a world which will never satisfy you: come unto Christ! Come, with all your sins, however many and however great,—however far you may have gone from God, and however provoking your conduct may have been. Come as you are: unfit, unmeet, unprepared as you may think yourself,—you will gain no fitness by delay. Come at once: come to the Lord Jesus Christ!

How indeed shall you escape if you neglect so great salvation? Where will you appear if you make light of the blood of Christ, and do despite to the Spirit of grace? It is a fearful thing to fall into the hands of the living God, but never so fearful as when men fall from under the Gospel. The saddest road to hell is that which runs under the pulpit, past the Bible, and through the midst of warnings and invitations. Oh, beware, lest like Israel at Kadesh, you mourn over your mistake when it is too late; or, like Judas Iscariot, find out your sin when there is no space for repentance.

Arise, and call upon the Lord. Be not like Esau: sell not eternal blessings for the things of to-day. Surely the time past may suffice you to have been careless and prayerless, Godless and Christless, worldly and earthly-minded. Surely the time to come may be given to your soul.

Pray, I beseech you, that you may be enabled to put off the old ways and the old habits, and that you may become a new man. I yield to none in wishes for your happiness, and my best wish is that you may be made a new creature in Christ Jesus. This is a better thing than riches, or health, or honour, or learning. A man may get to heaven without these, but he cannot get there without conversion. Verily if you die without having been born again you had far better never have been born at all. No man really lives till he lives unto God.

I leave my question with you. The Lord grant that it may prove a word in season to your soul. My heart's desire and prayer to God is that you may be saved. Awake, thou that sleepest, and arise from the dead, and Christ shall give thee light. Arise, O sleeper, and call upon God. There is yet hope. Forsake not thy mercies. Do not lose thine own soul.

The Publishers would welcome correspondence from any who have been helped by the reading of this book. *The Banner of Truth Trust* was formed in 1958, in order to assist, through literature, in the spread of the Christian Faith and the Gospel of Jesus Christ.

For free catalogue, write to:

THE BANNER OF TRUTH TRUST

3 Murrayfield Road, Edinburgh EH12 6EL

P.O. Box 621, Carlisle, Pennsylvania 17013, U.S.A.

RIGHT WITH GOD

John Blanchard

Some people know what Christianity is and reject it.
More do not know and do not wish to know. But there
are many who belong to neither of these classes. They
do not reject; they are not indifferent; yet they have not
found a personal knowledge of God. It is to help those
who thus search that this book has been written.
The author's first concern is to remove the main cause
of spiritual uncertainty, namely, ignorance of what the
Bible teaches. What this teaching is, as it concerns our
individual relation to God, is set out clearly, step by
step. And it leads positively to the Bible's own
conclusion, that salvation is free and undeserved and
received through the work of Jesus Christ, the Son of
God. 'For God sent not his Son into the world to
condemn the world; but that the world through him
might be saved.'

*John Blanchard was born in Guernsey in the Channel Islands in
1932. After thirteen years in the Guernsey Civil Service he has since
1965 been wholly engaged in a ministry of evangelism and Bible
Teaching.*

*Right With God, first published in 1971, has now sold over
quarter of a million copies throughout the English-speaking world.
It has been translated into more than a dozen languages, and is issued
in Braille by Torch Trust for the Blind, and on tape by Tape-Aids for
the Blind (South Africa).*